Surviving the Arctic Convoys

Surviving the Arctic Convoys

The Wartime Memoir of Leading Seaman Charlie Erswell

As told to

John R. McKay

Pen & Sword
MARITIME

First published in Great Britain in 2021 by
Pen & Sword Maritime
An imprint of
Pen & Sword Books Ltd
Yorkshire – Philadelphia

ISBN 978 1 39901 303 1

Printed and bound in the UK by CPI Group (UK) Ltd, Croydon, CR0 4YY.

Pen & Sword Books Limited incorporates the imprints of Atlas, Archaeology,
Aviation, Discovery, Family History, Fiction, History, Maritime, Military,
Military Classics, Politics, Select, Transport, True Crime, Air World, Frontline
Publishing, Leo Cooper, Remember When, Seaforth Publishing, The Praetorian
Press, Wharncliffe Local History, Wharncliffe Transport, Wharncliffe True
Crime and White Owl.

For a complete list of Pen & Sword titles please contact

PEN & SWORD BOOKS LIMITED
47 Church Street, Barnsley, South Yorkshire, S70 2AS, England
E-mail: enquiries@pen-and-sword.co.uk
Website: www.pen-and-sword.co.uk

Or
PEN AND SWORD BOOKS
1950 Lawrence Rd, Havertown, PA 19083, USA
E-mail: Uspen-and-sword@casematepublishers.com
Website: www.penandswordbooks.com

*For Betty Erswell, without whom
this book could never have been written.*

Contents

Acknowledgements

This book has been a labour of love. I have enjoyed every aspect of its production, from that first meeting with Charlie and Betty in December 2019, to the endless exchange of emails that have flown almost daily back and forth between us in the process of completing the manuscript.

I would like to thank the following people for their contribution to the book: my brother Paul McKay and ex-US Navy sailor David Samaras, for offering their thoughts and advice on the early drafts; my wife Dawn for her encouragement and love and also for supporting me on the original decision to embark on the project. I would also like to thank Ian Martin of the KOSB Museum in Berwick-upon-Tweed and Anne Moore, Keeper of Collections at Northumberland Museums, for assistance with some of the research. Thanks go to Keith Nisbet Photography, Woking for permission to use a photograph.

Thanks to all at Pen & Sword, primarily Matt Jones, George Chamier and, in particular, Henry Wilson, who agrees with me that it is historically important that the stories of these men should be told.

The following books have proved invaluable in my research:

Peter C. Brown, *Voices from the Arctic Convoys*
Vice-Admiral Sir Ian Campbell & Captain Donald McIntyre, *The Kola Run*
Bernard Edwards, *The Road To Russia: Arctic Convoys 1942–45*
Peter C. Smith, *Convoy PQ18 – Arctic Victory*
Michael G. Walling, *Forgotten Sacrifice – The Arctic Convoys of World War 2*

However, most valuable of all has been the time I have spent with Charlie, during which he has regaled me with tales of his time at sea. So a huge thank you to Charlie Erswell, ex-Leading Seaman/Gunner RN, for letting me tell his story.

My final (huge) debt of thanks goes to Charlie's wife, Betty. I am fully aware of my incessant haranguing of her for information and I know that she has spent many hours in front of her computer screen replying to my constant stream of emails. She has done this with immense good cheer, and I will be forever grateful for the time, effort and love she has put into this project. Without Betty, this book could never have been written. The book is therefore deservedly dedicated to her.

For more information on the Arctic Convoys please take a look at the website of the Russian Arctic Convoy Project, a museum dedicated to the convoys in Aultbea, near Loch Ewe in Scotland. www.racmp.co.uk

For more information on all my work: www.johnrmckay.com

Introduction

I first met Charlie Erswell and his wonderful wife, Betty, just before Christmas 2019. They had contacted me by email to offer praise, which was greatly appreciated, for my Arctic convoy novel, *The Worst Journey in the World*. They happened to mention that if I was ever passing Wakefield I would be very welcome to pop in for a cup of tea and a chat. Charlie informed me that he had served on HMS *Milne* and HMS *Savage* during the Second World War, both ships having sailed in numerous convoys to Russia and across the Atlantic.

Coincidentally, I was due to visit my brother-in-law in Mansfield the following weekend, and so, on our return home, my wife Dawn and I paid them a visit.

It truly was an honour to meet them both, and the stories Charlie told me of his time aboard the two destroyers got me thinking once again about the Arctic convoys and how recognition of what happened during those voyages has faded over the years. As Charlie says, no films have been made about those voyages, and the literary world has also ignored the chance to tell such amazing tales of adventure and heroism.

In fact, it is not only the entertainment industry that has overlooked the story of the convoys; successive governments have too. It took a long time, nearly seventy years, before the British government recognized these brave men's achievements in that theatre of war, with the award of the Arctic Star. Prior to this, they had only been allowed to wear a lapel pin and a white beret to indicate they were veterans of the Arctic convoys. Cynically, it might be suggested the new award had only come about after Britain was upstaged by the Russian government awarding those sailors the Ushakov medal in 2014.

After hearing Charlie's story, I suggested we collaborate and write his autobiography, as a way to record his recollections of those times for posterity. I was extremely pleased that he agreed to this. The following pages are a story of a life well lived, a life that could very easily have been cut short on many occasions by the sea, diphtheria, Nazi bombs and torpedoes and, on one or two other occasions, by misadventure!

You could describe him as an ex-gunner on HMS *Milne* and HMS *Savage,* or simply as a veteran of the Second World War, but to do so would not do justice to the man's service record, and so it deserves to be given in detail. He is a veteran of ten Arctic convoys (in both directions); he is a veteran of the Battle of the Atlantic; he is a veteran of Operation Torch; he is a veteran of D-Day; he is a veteran of the liberation of Norway. He is all of those things. And what makes it doubly impressive is that he was not conscripted. He volunteered for it all and was only eighteen years old when he first went to war.

Charlie is the recipient of many medals, including: the 1939–45 Star, The Atlantic Star, The Arctic Star, The North Africa Star, British Campaign Medal, D-Day Veterans Medal, Légion d'Honneur, Ushakov medal (Russia), and the Soviet 40 year Jubilee Medal.

What comes across strongly of Charlie is his humour, humility and sense of fun. Had I been of the same generation, I would like to think we could very easily have been mates. I can just imagine going 'on the lash' with him in the bars of Gibraltar, Naples and Valletta. In essence, he is just a normal bloke who has done a lot of extraordinary things in his life, many tales of which are now recorded in the following pages.

It has been an honour and privilege to have been able to record his story.

John R. McKay
Wigan, 2020

Prologue

13 September 1942 – Barents Sea, south-west of Spitzbergen

We had been closed up at 'action stations' since crossing the Arctic Circle, and the temperature was now at an unbearable 25º below zero. Sleet and rain filled the air around us, as it had done for the past few days, but the fog that had seemed to follow us since leaving Iceland had now lifted. We were at a heightened state of alert and had been since we set sail from Hvalfjödur four days ago.

Suddenly, the tannoy broke the silence and a voice I recognized as one of the officers on the bridge informed us there were forty-four torpedo bombers approaching the convoy from the starboard side.

'Can I see?' asked the breech loader, leaning over my shoulder, grabbing my telescope and putting it to his eye.

'They're not planes,' he declared after a moment. 'They're birds.'

From a distance they did indeed look like a flock of birds. There was no denying it. But out here, in the frozen wastes of the Arctic Ocean, they couldn't be anything other than what the officer had told us over the tannoy. He just did not want to believe it.

This was clearly the Luftwaffe heading towards us, flying in line abreast no more than 200ft above the waves, the drone of their engines getting ever louder the closer they came; Junkers Ju-88s and Heinkel He-111s flying in tight formation. Almost fifty of them, each carrying two torpedoes and bearing down on us to attack the merchant vessels we were there to protect.

I pulled my mittens tight and flexed my fingers. Despite the cold, I felt confident. I was ready for them. After the brief skirmishes we had thus far endured, this was definitely something much bigger. But I felt fully prepared, determined and ready to do a good job.

From my position inside the turret I was able to take a brief look around me. Outside, as far as my eyes could see, grey skies looked down upon a choppy ocean. To the port side, many merchant ships laboriously sailed on through the ice floes, burdened with the weight of their vital cargoes. They relied totally on sailors just like me to protect them from the coming assault. I was aware that the men on those ships looked to us in the Royal Navy to keep them safe, their own pitiful defences being totally inadequate to deal with a concerted aerial assault.

To the north, beyond the convoy, through the sleet and rain I could just make out the silhouettes of huge icebergs. Like leviathans they observed us indifferently, the battle that was about to take place before them of no real concern.

As the gun trainer, it was my job to turn the turret in the direction of the enemy planes, whilst the gun layer raised and lowered the long barrels of the 4.7 inch guns. We followed the instructions of the Petty Officer, who received his orders from the director above the bridge. We were to line up the pointers as indicated, and then the breech loaders would pump shells into the guns and fire them at the approaching aircraft.

Although this was something we had been trained to do and had so far done well, the sheer number of the approaching planes made my heart beat faster, and I swear I could feel the blood pumping around my veins, warming me slightly despite the horrendous cold we were all having to contend with.

I grabbed the winding handles, my concentration now totally focused on the task ahead.

We had to prevent the Ju-88s and He-111s from dropping their loads. Each of those planes carried enough firepower to sink two ships. They simply had to be stopped. And we were the ones tasked to stop them.

A metal bucket was on the floor near to me, for anyone who might suffer from seasickness since, being at 'action stations', we were unable to leave our positions to go outside and throw up. I was fortunate enough not to suffer from that particular malady, but the stench the bucket gave off, whenever my shipmates were forced to make use of it, only added to the general discomfort of operating in such a confined space.

I took a breath and readied myself. No sooner had I settled than the order was given to open fire.

We worked methodically, turning the turret and fixing on the targets as they approached. The breech loaders worked furiously, pumping shell after shell into the guns and firing them skyward, where they exploded amongst the approaching aircraft. The noise was horrendous as each shot was fired, the breech shooting back to eject the empty shell cases on to the floor around us. The smell of cordite filled the turret, the smoke mixing with the condensation from our breath as we worked furiously to repel the attack.

Above this din the Petty Officer shouted his orders, and we had to strain our ears to hear him. Our concentration could not lapse for a single moment.

As I wound the handles back and forth, lining up the pointer on the targets, we could clearly hear the sound of the engines in the German planes as they swooped down to drop their deadly ordnance. All around us was the sound of explosions, mixed with the unmistakable noise of the 'pom-poms', Oerlikons and machine guns, as the weapons from all the ships of the screen joined the aerial barrage.

I continued to follow the pointers as the range was adjusted, listening intently to the Petty Officer's orders. More explosions filled my ears, closer this time, and I had a feeling of dread that things were not going well out there. Had some of the planes got through? Had some of the ships been hit?

I could not think about that right now. I had to keep going, despite the cold that was trying to numb my body, the elements trying to stop me from carrying out my duty.

I shivered. It was all so very cold. I never knew temperatures could go this low. It was incessant. I feared that if the Germans did not do for me, then the cold of the Arctic would.

However, we had to put that fear to one side and carry on.

For our comrades depended on us.

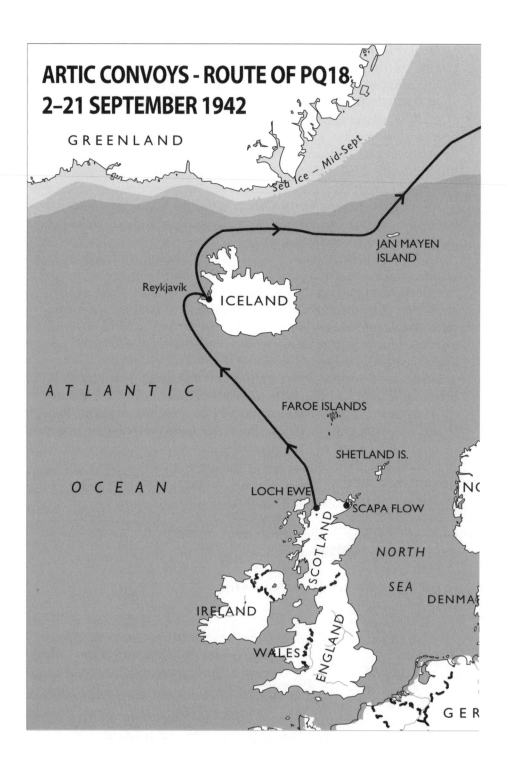

ARTIC CONVOYS - ROUTE OF PQ18
2–21 SEPTEMBER 1942

GREENLAND

Sea Ice – Mid-Sept

JAN MAYEN
ISLAND

Reykjavík

ICELAND

ATLANTIC

FAROE ISLANDS

SHETLAND IS.

OCEAN

LOCH EWE

SCAPA FLOW

NO

NORTH

SCOTLAND

SEA

DENMA

IRELAND

WALES

ENGLAND

GER

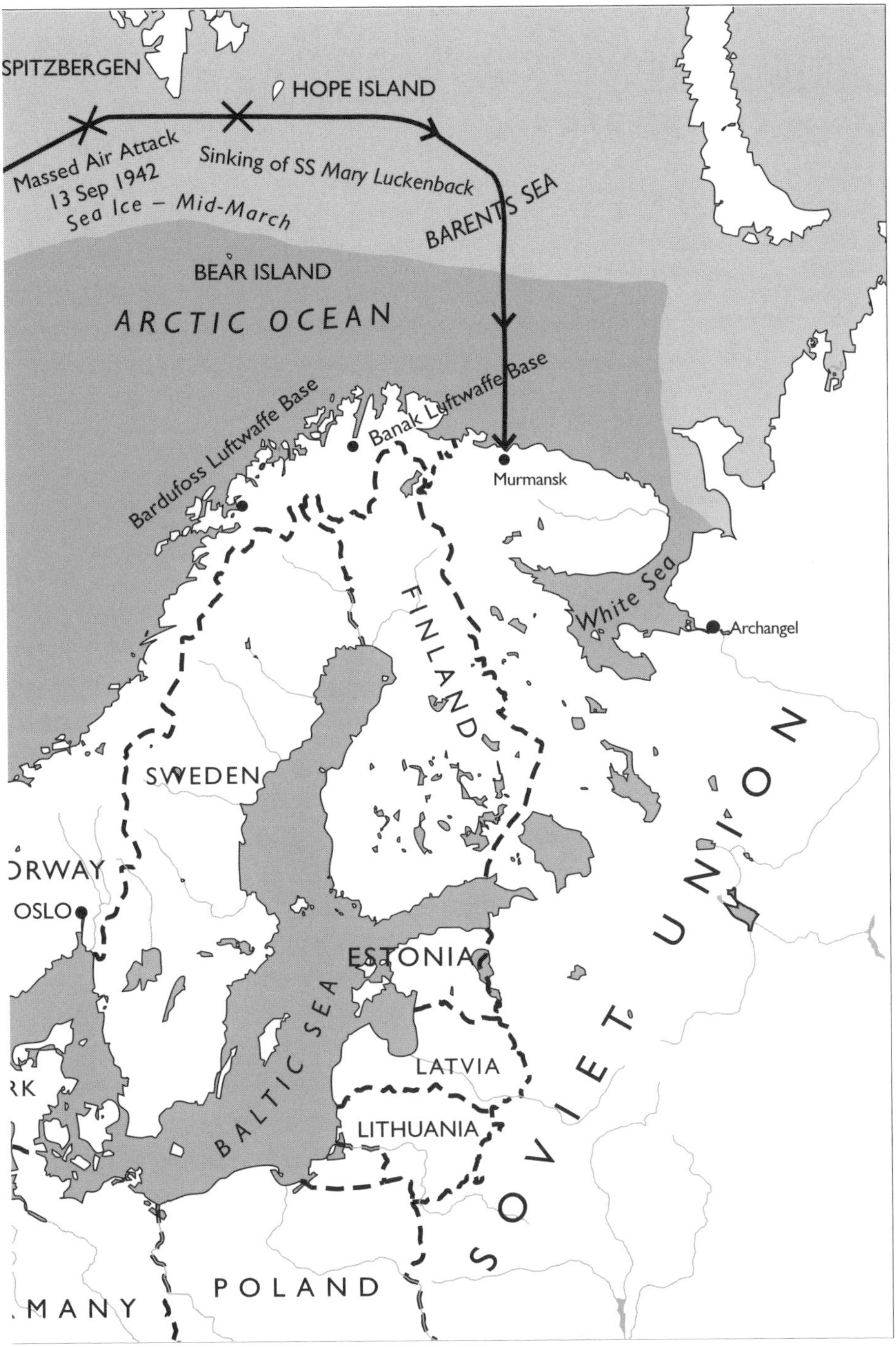

SPITZBERGEN

HOPE ISLAND

Massed Air Attack
13 Sep 1942
Sea Ice – Mid-March

Sinking of SS Mary Luckenback

BARENTS SEA

BEAR ISLAND

ARCTIC OCEAN

Bardufoss Luftwaffe Base

Banak Luftwaffe Base

Murmansk

White Sea

Archangel

FINLAND

SWEDEN

NORWAY

OSLO

ESTONIA

SOVIET UNION

BALTIC SEA

LATVIA

LITHUANIA

DENMARK

GERMANY

POLAND

CHAPTER ONE

Growing up In Berwick

Berwick-upon-Tweed is well known as the coldest town in England. It lies in Northumberland at the mouth of the Tweed, where the river flows into the North Sea. Less than three miles south of the Scottish border, it is exposed to the north-east winds that come straight from the Arctic, bringing with them temperatures below freezing in the winter and cooler summers than most of the rest of Great Britain.

In 1928, this small, picturesque town was home to my family, the Erswells, and on 16 May of that year, Edward, Prince of Wales (the future King Edward VIII) visited the town to open a new bridge across the river. The 'old bridge' as it was known, was no longer fit for purpose, being only wide enough for one-way traffic, meaning any vehicle had to wait until anything approaching had first passed. To solve this problem, the Royal Tweed Bridge, a modern, wider structure, was built, and when Prince Edward came to officially open it there was huge excitement in the town.

Bunting hung from buildings and street lamps, and crowds lined the roads, the townspeople eager to get a glimpse of the young royal as he executed his duties. The sense of patriotism abounded, the feeling of Britishness apparent. After all, it had not been ten years since Britain had emerged victorious from the Great War, proving she was still the most formidable nation on the planet.

Standing on this new bridge as a very young child, I joined the schoolchildren in singing 'God Bless the Prince of Wales' as I watched the procession go by, not really understanding what the whole thing was about. All I knew was that it was an exciting time and somebody important was visiting our small town. I smiled and waved my Union flag along with the rest of the children, enjoying the excitement of the celebration. When the well-dressed gentleman exited the car and stood alongside other dignitaries to officially declare the bridge open, I did not realize how important an historical figure I was looking at. This was the man who would one day be King of England and then go through the controversial process of giving it all up for the love of a divorced American woman.

The two bridges that now spanned the Tweed gave rise to a tradition. Each summer, races were held in which young men from the town would jump from the old bridge and swim up the river to the Royal Tweed Bridge, an occasion enjoyed by the whole community until the number of fatalities caused by the practice caused it to be scrapped, and it eventually faded away into history.

* * *

Infant mortality in 1920s and 1930s Britain was one in twenty. Five per cent of babies born at that time could expect not to see their first birthday. Every year, thousands died of infectious diseases such as pneumonia, meningitis, tuberculosis and polio. Poor diet and bad living conditions were the root cause of much of this childhood illness, and one of the biggest causes of infant death during that period was diphtheria, the symptoms of which are akin to influenza. High temperatures, a nasal discharge, a thick grey membrane that covered a very sore throat, and swollen lymph glands were just some of the manifestations a sick child would have to endure when suffering from it. This awful disease caused the deaths of many poor children unlucky enough to contract it.

A few short miles outside of Berwick, two of my young cousins were to fall to the disease. This happened at the same time that I myself lay suffering in an isolation hospital, fighting for my own survival. Being of very small stature, it was feared that, like my cousins, I would not live through the epidemic and would perish along with them.

But even at the tender age of four, I, Charles George Francis Erswell, was made of stronger stuff than most.

Born in Stevenston, Ayrshire on 4 December 1923 to an ex-soldier and an Italian mother, I was the younger of two siblings, my sister Annette being three years older. My father, Harry Erswell, had been a career soldier, serving for many years as a Conductor (warrant officer), detached from the British to the Indian Army, before being posted to Alexandria, Egypt. There he met his wife, my mother, Guiseppina Chiricello, a young widow from Pozzuoli, near Naples. After a whirlwind courtship, Harry brought her back to Britain on his final posting to the King's Own Scottish Borderers' regimental headquarters in Berwick-upon-Tweed. Once this tour of duty was completed and he was discharged from the Army, together with his family he took up the lease of a public house, The George Inn, on Church Street, in the heart of the town.

In the isolation hospital the doctors did not hold out much hope for my survival. Left alone for hours on end, I would amuse myself by killing the cockroaches that crawled over the floor and my bed, bashing them with the toy rifle I had been given by my parents. Mother and father were only able to visit me occasionally, due to fear of contamination, and they were not allowed to enter my room, having to settle for waving to me through the window.

Ironically, seeing my mother through this small piece of glass would be the last memory I would ever have of her, as she was to pass away during my confinement. This left my father and grandmother, Emma Louise Judge, to raise us two children when I returned home after my quite unexpected recovery.

After the death of our mother, Annette and I were pretty much left to our own devices. Able to wander the town and surrounding countryside at will, we took advantage of the freedom our father allowed us and explored and enjoyed all Berwick had to offer. Being inquisitive by nature, I would often roam around the battlements and watch the fishing boats on the Tweed as they brought in their hauls to sell at the local markets and towns beyond. This gave rise to a fascination with all things nautical, and even at this early age I knew where my destiny lay. Looking across the bay and out to the North Sea, the Berwick lighthouse to the right, I often dreamed of the day I would set sail and explore the seven seas, imagining all the adventures I would have when I was older.

In this small town of around 12,000 inhabitants, the walk to school was only a few hundred yards. The Boys' British School at the end of Ravensdowne was where I received my early schooling, and the windows of the classroom on the top floor gave me a wonderful view of the lighthouse, the sea and, on a clear day, the town of Spittal to the south.

It was on just such a warm, sunny day that I sat at my desk allowing my mind to wander. I gazed longingly out of the window, wishing I was out there, sitting on the old cannons on Berwick's battlements and enjoying the sunshine and the great outdoors.

Suddenly a cane swooshed down and cracked on my desk to the side of me, making me jump and jolting me from my day-dreams. This was a tactic of the headmaster's to gain the attention of pupils who were prone to the odd lapse of concentration. And with the further threat of a whack of the cane across our back-sides, it had the desired effect of ensuring we never did it more than once.

If there was one thing all of us feared, it was the wrath of the headmaster and his vicious stick. I had so far been lucky to avoid it, but many in the classroom had experienced just what the old teacher was threatening. The man ruled the school with an iron fist and would not tolerate inattention during his lessons.

Eventually, the bell rang for lunch and the classroom emptied. Some of the children headed to the Town Hall, where a soup kitchen had been set up at the rear. Many families could not afford to send their children to school with food, or money for dinner, and so the soup kitchen was their only chance of a decent meal during the day. However, I was one of the lucky ones. My father made enough money to feed and clothe me and my sister well. But for others, times were proving harder. From the first floor window of the George Inn, I watched my schoolmates queuing patiently for their dinner. Some of my friends wore garments that had clearly been handed down from older siblings, threadbare and torn in places, and their shoes had holes which let in water and snow during inclement weather.

Summer in Berwick was always the best of times, especially during the school holidays. It was a chance for us children to have fun and, if we were savvy enough, to make some decent pocket money.

Often my friends and I would go down to the local golf course, where we would search for missing balls and then sell them back to the golfers who had been unlucky enough to lose them. How the balls came to be lost in the first place was not always down to bad play, and although the gentlemen went along with our banter, we understood they really knew not all the balls had been acquired completely honestly. However, they were willing to hand over a few coppers to get them back, and it always ended in smiles, with both parties coming out of the transaction feeling they had got the best out of the deal.

On Saturdays in summertime it was always prudent to hang around St Andrews and other churches. There was a tradition at the time that newly wedded couples would throw silver coins to the local children outside the church, and we were able to pick up extra pocket money this way. There was always a mad scramble for the coins, and this could result in arguments amongst our group when one of us felt we had not done as well as we had hoped. However, the money was usually divided equally and we all were quite happy. Once we were sure we had all there was available, we ran off once more to play elsewhere in the town.

I had a love of the battlements that circled the town and would spend a lot of time on them. This was my favourite place of all. From here I could look out to the sea that seemed to be calling to me, beckoning me, persuading me my future lay out there on the water. The air was clear and, although it was cold, this did not bother me at all. After surviving diphtheria I felt I could endure anything. A little cold did not trouble me in the slightest.

One day, when I got home after spending some time at the battlements, dreaming of a life at sea, I spoke to my father who was sitting quietly at the kitchen table.

'I think I'm going to join the Navy when I'm older,' I declared.

Harry Erswell looked up from the newspaper he was reading. 'You'll do no such thing,' he replied. 'It's the Army for you, my boy.'

'I don't want to join the Army. I want to go on a ship,' I responded.

My father folded the paper and put it down on the table. 'That's not going to happen, Charles. We're a family of soldiers. My father was a soldier and his father was one before him. So you, young man, are also going to be a soldier. It's what we Erswells do.'

I frowned. One thing I did not want to be was a soldier! The very idea of it went against all I felt. No matter what my father said, I was determined one day I was to be a sailor. And not just any sailor. I was going to be the best one the British Navy ever had.

*   *   *

Each Sunday, Annette and I were ordered to have a bath before morning service, which we were forced to attend (before Sunday school and then evening service). It was on one such day, after Annette had been bathed and dressed in her best clothes, that she and I had cross words. We would bicker, as siblings do, and, being the elder, she would let me know where I stood in the pecking order. As I was getting out of the bath she accosted me, taunting me about how I was the 'little favourite' and could do no wrong.

Being so young, I quickly became upset at her sneering as she told me how I was just a silly little boy and she was much better than I.

I asked her to stop teasing, but when she ignored me and carried on, I let my frustration get the better of me and gave her the hardest shove I could muster. Taken by surprise, Annette staggered backwards and fell against the bathtub. Despite her desperate attempts to stop herself, she fell full length into the tub with an almighty splash.

Quickly she scrambled out, soaked to the skin, her best clothes dripping wet with dirty bathwater. Suddenly our father came rushing into the room, demanding to know what all the fuss was about.

'It's Charlie,' said Annette, through tear-filled eyes. 'He's just pushed me into the bath.'

Turning to me, my father demanded why on earth I had done such a thing.

By now, unable to control my tears, I told him she had been teasing me, to which Annette denied having done anything wrong.

My tears turned to sobs as I saw my father take the belt from around his waist.

'Come here, young man,' he said. 'You need to be taught a lesson.'

* * *

My fascination with the sea grew as the seasons passed.

One day in 1929, when only six years old, I looked down at the small fishing boats bobbing at their moorings in Marshall's Cove, a small inlet on the coast. I loved going down there with Annette; with our friends, we would have fun jumping from the hand-holds on the cliff face on to the soft sand below. Close by, a number of rowing boats floated on the water, secured by ropes to a stone jetty. These were used by the fishermen to get to their trawlers and fishing boats which were moored further out to sea.

This particular day, I looked at my sister, hoping to avoid her scrutiny. She seemed absorbed in the fun she was having with her friends, taking no notice of me at all. Seeing the opportunity, I slowly made my way along the jetty towards the boats to get a better look. I looked out across the expanse of water that stretched to the horizon beyond the river which split the town in two. I remember gazing out in wonder, my young imagination conjuring up images and dreams of what lay beyond the limit of my vision. What strange and wonderful places were out there? What adventures I could have if only I could get on board one of those fishing boats moored further out, and take it out to sea.

The nearest rowing boat had drifted a few feet away, pulling the rope that held it taut. If I could just get inside it and row out to the bigger boats then I could take a look inside one. I felt compelled to find out what they contained.

My curiosity now fully aroused, I bent down, gripped the rope and pulled. I was astonished to find that, despite my young age and small size, the little boat moved towards me quite easily, gliding effortlessly across the short stretch of water. Smiling to myself, I realized all it needed was another tug and the boat would be up against the jetty and I would be able to get on board.

Without warning, there was a sudden surge in the water and the boat lifted on a wave before being pulled back away from the jetty.

Taken completely by surprise, and still holding the rope, I was pulled off the jetty, before tumbling headfirst into the water.

I could not swim!

Taking in a mouthful of salt water, I honestly thought this was it. Where diphtheria had failed, the sea I was so fond of was about to succeed and do for me. I started to panic. I could not feel the seabed beneath my feet and although I had managed to get my head out of the water, my inability to swim meant I quickly sank below the surface again.

I realized I was drowning.

After what seemed an age, I felt strong arms grab hold of me, and with a huge effort I was hoisted clear of the water and back on to the jetty. Coughing and spluttering and spitting out salty sea water, the panic of dying slowly left me and I was able to look up and see who had just saved my life.

Annette, now also soaked to the skin, looked down at her brother, the tears in her eyes mingling with the salt water, her hair plastered to her head and face.

'You silly little beggar,' she sniffled. 'What were you playing at? You could have drowned.'

I had never been so pleased to see my sister in all of my life.

'One thing you need to do, Charlie,' she said later, when we had got our breath back and were returning home. 'You need to learn how to swim!'

The misadventure at the cove did not put me off water. For most young people it would have probably given them a fear of it for a very long time, if not forever. But not I. The incident made me realize my sister was right. I did need to learn how to swim, and the sooner that was done the better. After all, if I was going to be a sailor when I grew up, surely being able to swim was something of a prerequisite.

And so, together with my friend Jim Renton, the son of the local dairy farmer, I set off to an open air pool near to the sea's edge, not far from the cove where I nearly drowned, to learn how to do it, this time under supervision. After each lesson, as we walked home, we enjoyed a sandwich which was known accurately as a 'Shivery Bite'.

During high winds, which were a regular occurrence, ice-cold seawater would often spray into the pool and over us swimmers. This did not put me off in any way and I was soon an able, if not technical, swimmer, my style of six over-arm strokes followed by a sort of 'scrabbling about' enough to make me feel confident in the water. By the age of ten I was able to swim across the bay quite easily, my confidence having grown exponentially. This acclimatization and indifference to the cold would prove a good training ground for my future life and voyages to the Arctic.

*   *   *

In 1933, my father's tenancy of the George Inn came to an end. Unable to afford the lease any longer, he sought work elsewhere and was offered a job by an old acquaintance, working for the Legion of Frontiersmen, at its headquarters just off the Strand in London. Founded in 1905, shortly after the Boer War, the Legion of Frontiersmen was an organization that recruited people throughout the British Empire to prepare civilians for war and to protect the boundaries of the Empire's territories. Many of its members were former soldiers and adventurers, and branches were established throughout the world, but ultimately, the Legion would fail to gain the official recognition its leaders craved.

And so, when I was ten years old, the family was forced to move away from the town we had grown to love, and we all made the journey to a new life in Hornchurch, Essex.

CHAPTER TWO

The Blitz

At around the same time that we were upping sticks and moving into our new home on Warriner Avenue in Hornchurch, the world around us was taking on a new and sinister turn. In Germany, a new Chancellor had come to power, a man who had risen from almost nowhere to put an end to the Weimar Republic and the old way of doing things. The ex-corporal promised a new and greater Germany, free from the restrictions of the Versailles Treaty, and promised to make it a major European force once more. This man, of course, was Adolf Hitler.

With the rise of the National Socialist Workers (Nazi) Party, and with Hitler now in charge, the country's conversion to a dictatorship happened swiftly and ruthlessly. The infamous Night of the Long Knives cut any resistance to his authority, and it was not long before the Nazis had total power over the whole country, controlling all aspects of German life. A clash with other major powers was inevitable. It was just a matter of time.

To a 10-year-old boy politics was of no real concern. This was a subject adults talked about and it held no interest for me. I was much more focused on settling into my new school and making new friends. It had been a wrench to move from Berwick, as the time I had spent there, although tough on occasion, had been a happy one, filled with fun, adventure and freedom. Even at that young age I knew I would miss it and would always have fond memories of my early childhood there.

My father enrolled me in the new Drury Falls Secondary Modern School, and I settled into my new environment quickly. Not so Dickensian as the school I attended in Berwick, ruled with an almost iron fist by its headmaster, Drury Falls was much less strict. It was not long before I was proving to be a conscientious and hard-working pupil, liked by both the staff and my peers.

I was not necessarily the most academic of pupils, and it quickly became clear that my strengths lay elsewhere. It was during an assembly when I came to realize my talents were more of a sporting nature rather than a scholastic, or indeed, a musical one. One morning, whilst singing along to a hymn with the rest of the children, I was rudely led away by one of the teachers and deposited at the back of the assembly hall, with instructions to take no further part in the song being sung. To my own ear I thought I had sounded all right, even good, but the opinion of those listening was quite the opposite. Without noticing, I had reached that age when my voice had broken, and instead of achieving the high notes the song required, a more bass, tuneless sound had exited my vocal chords.

Seeing me sitting twiddling my thumbs at the rear of the room, doing my best to comply with the order I had been given, the sports teacher approached and asked if I would rather join a class in the gymnasium. The music teacher offered no objection, and so I was willingly conscripted into the sports squad.

The school had excellent facilities for most sports, including football and cricket pitches and an athletics track, but it was in the gymnasium where I excelled. Being of small stature and with a naturally low centre of gravity, I became a talented gymnast and an expert at climbing ropes. And despite my size, I excelled in the 110m hurdles.

The years passed, and just before my fourteenth birthday I again broached with my father the subject of joining the Navy. He was not impressed. He told me the Army was the place for me and it could offer me a good life and a career with plenty of opportunity for foreign travel. After all, he himself had spent many years travelling the world, from India to Egypt and many places in between. He had even met my mother on his travels with the Army. He explained that with his own service record it would be easy to get me taken on as an apprentice armourer, and this was where I should focus my future.

But I was not for persuading. In my mind I was already committed to the Royal Navy. There was no way I would be talked out of it. My mind was set and I let my feelings be known. I was no longer prepared to discuss joining the Army when I was older.

Sighing, my father relented, and a few days later, on my fourteenth birthday, he reluctantly took me to the local Royal Navy recruiting office to see if I could enlist as a boy entrant.

Leaving my father to wait for me in the reception area, I followed the recruiting officer down a narrow stairway into a dusty basement, where I was told to sit at a table. An unshaded bulb hung loosely from the ceiling, providing a dim light and leaving the two of us in almost semi-darkness. There then followed an interview of sorts, in which I was asked about my interests, schooling and aspirations. This lasted no more than ten minutes before I was taken for an eye test, and upon its completion was told to rejoin my father. It all happened very quickly.

A few moments later, the recruiting officer approached us both.

'Hello, Charles . . . Mr Erswell,' he said, matter-of-factly. 'It's bad news. Unfortunately, you've failed the eye test, young man. We can't accept you into the service, I'm afraid. Sorry about that.'

With that, he turned on his heel and walked away.

'Don't worry, lad,' said my father, placing his hand on my shoulder sympathetically as we gathered our things and left the building. 'Give it a couple of years and you can maybe try for the Army instead.'

There is no denying I was upset. All my dreams had come crashing down around me. Would I ever get to be a sailor? Would I ever fulfil my dream of sailing the seas? No matter what my father said, I still had no intention of following in his footsteps and becoming a soldier.

As we walked away from the recruiting office, heading for home, I looked at my father. Was that a smirk on his face? Had he had a hand in this failure? I could not be sure and so put the thought to the back of my mind. I realized I was still very young, and maybe another opportunity would present itself in the future. There was no point worrying about it now. I fully understood my father would probably never sign for me to join the Navy. I realized if I was to fulfil my ambition and go to sea, then I would probably have to wait until I was eighteen and sign up for myself.

Instead of joining the Navy as a boy recruit, I had to settle for a job as a telegram delivery boy with the General Post Office (GPO) in the City of London, a job I acquired through my sister, who also worked for them. Based at various locations throughout the city, including the Headquarters at Cannon Street and King

Edward Street near to St Paul's Cathedral, I made the hour-long trip to work each day and sometimes stayed on the premises overnight to avoid the journey back if I was on an early shift the following morning.

As I settled into the routine of early adult life, the world around me was becoming more and more unstable. By the summer of 1939 it was clear to most that war with Germany was coming ever closer. The Nazis had continually defied the Treaty of Versailles and were showing a complete disregard for the international community. On 12 March the previous year the Wehrmacht marched across the border into Austria and annexed the whole country (this was the '*Anschluss*'), absorbing it into the Greater German Empire. With tensions mounting in Europe, war had looked to have been averted that September at the Munich conference, when on the final day the Prime Minister, Neville Chamberlain, persuaded Hitler to sign a piece of paper agreeing never to go to war with Britain. This note he waved enthusiastically to the press on the runway at Halton aerodrome upon his return, heralding the achievement of 'peace in our time'. (On the very same day that Chamberlain arrived back from Munich, I was called upon to deliver a telegram to the Prime Minister at No. 10 Downing Street!)

Although agreement had been reluctantly reached in Munich for the Germans to annex the Sudetenland, the Czech territory on Germany's southern border, they nevertheless invaded the rest of Czechoslovakia in March 1939.

Less than six months later, on 1 September, an unprovoked Germany unexpectedly invaded Poland. Given an ultimatum by Britain to withdraw his troops or face war, Hitler ignored the demand, and on 3 September Britain and France declared war on Germany.

To me, sixteen year-old Charlie Erswell, telegram boy for the GPO in London, this would prove to be a momentous and fateful day, even if I did not know it just yet.

*   *   *

Still too young to join the armed forces, I looked for some other military role to fill the gap before I could. With war now declared, the frustration I felt that I was not old enough to 'do my bit' was eating at me, and it was with great delight that a friend and I discovered an Army Cadet Unit operating nearby in the Old Stock Exchange: the 1st Cadet Battalion, Royal Fusiliers. The unit trained every week and, as the age for joining was fifteen and a half, it was an ideal opportunity for us to gain some experience. I just hoped the war would not be over before I had a chance to go and fight for real. The unit was run by a First World War veteran, the wonderfully named Max Karo.

Max Karo was a wealthy stockbroker and philanthropist. Born in Russia in 1876, he emigrated to London at the age of twenty and became a British citizen in 1902, the year after Queen Victoria's death. He worked in the City of London and became a successful stockbroker at the London Stock Exchange in 1909. At the age of thirty-eight, he volunteered for the Army at the outbreak of the First World War and served with the 26th Battalion Royal Fusiliers (Bankers) in France, until transferring to the 38th Battalion as an instructor. After the war he was commissioned into the Jewish Lads Brigade and later founded the Stock Exchange Cadet Company as part of the Army Cadet Force.

It was Karo himself who interviewed me when I applied to join the company, and I was delighted to be accepted. I was given a uniform, funded from Karo's own pocket, which was basically a First World War tunic, peaked cap and puttees. We boys affectionately referred to ourselves as 'Max Karo's Army'. The Company also had its own band, who wore blue patrol jackets and Busby hats like the Guards who looked after them; their music reached a very high standard .

The drill instructors came from the Guards Brigades, Chelsea Barracks. Sergeants from the Scots, Irish, Grenadier and Coldstream Guards took turns instructing the cadets in drill and field exercises, designed to reach a standard that would give us cadets a chance at enlisting in officer training school once we were old enough.

Karo took a personal interest in all of his cadets, getting to know us individually and offering advice and guidance. He also helped some to find jobs.

The time I spent with the unit gave me a very good grounding for the training I was to experience a couple of years later.

Throughout the rest of 1939 and into 1940, I continued working for the GPO and spent evenings with my friends and comrades of 'Max Karo's Army'. However, the news from France was not good. After months with almost no military activity, the 'Phoney War' came to an abrupt end at the beginning of May 1940, when the German Army advanced almost unexpectedly into France. Taken by surprise, the Allies were quickly overwhelmed and the British Expeditionary Force retreated westward to the coast, congregating at Dunkirk, where over 300,000 soldiers were famously evacuated from the beaches.

At work, I was now issued with an official steel helmet and gas mask container. In the main, the telegrams I delivered before the conflict were of a mundane nature, information being passed between various businesses in the City, with the occasional foray to other establishments including the Tower of London to deliver messages to soldiers barracked there. This was more exciting, because the messengers had to go into the Tower to find the soldier concerned, personally hand him the telegram and await a reply, should one be required. As the return message was dictated, my colleagues and I would price up the cost and collect the money, unless it was a 'reply paid' telegram. This gave us boys an excuse for taking our time getting back to the office for another delivery, a practice that became known as 'miking'.

However, with the outbreak of war, telegram messengers became associated with the delivery of bad news, and each of us boys dreaded getting a war casualty telegram to deliver to a bereaved family.

It was clear now the conflict could not be won any time soon, if at all. Britain was the only country able to fight the Germans, and that fight was clearly being lost. The threat of invasion was very real and a sense of nervousness permeated the country. It was not long before the Germans pushed ahead with 'Operation Sealion', their plan for the invasion of Britain, the first phase of which was to nullify the threat of the Royal Air Force.

Throughout the summer of 1940, dogfights could be seen in the skies above London and the South East, as the Luftwaffe fought to take command of the air.

Without aerial superiority no invasion of Britain would be possible. Whereas on land the German Blitzkrieg powered forward, vanquishing any army in their way, for the war in the air the story was very different. The pilots of the RAF, despite being outnumbered, managed to defeat the might of the German Luftwaffe, and after months of fighting in the skies the Nazi hierarchy came to realize an invasion of Great Britain was not going to be feasible.

My own personal experience of the Battle of Britain, besides observing the dogfights in the skies during that long hot summer, came one evening in Hornchurch.

Each Sunday, my best friend, Arthur Hadley, invited me to his home for tea. Arthur's story was similar to my own in that he had lost a parent at a very young age and now lived with his house-bound mother. We were the same age, our birthdays both falling in December.

In the late summer of 1940 I once again found myself at my friend's house. We planned to go to the cinema that evening. After we had eaten a wonderfully cooked roast dinner, Arthur's mother took to the piano, where she played classical music effortlessly. Being a lover of most music, I enjoyed watching her fingers glide across the keys, losing herself in the notes she so expertly created. I was fascinated at how skilfully she had mastered the instrument, the notes almost perfect, the whole thing a joy to my ears.

After a while Arthur got to his feet and found his coat, telling me we had to get a move on if we were to make the start of the film.

Slowly I stood up, still absorbing the wonderful music my friend's mother was producing, until she finally stopped playing and bade us goodnight. As we left the house I promised to come back the following week. Having lost my own mother at such a young age, those Sunday afternoons were something I always looked forward to.

A couple of hours later, having enjoyed a film at the Odeon, we were walking along Station Lane when we heard an almighty whining noise above our heads.

Instinctively, we both ducked. Then, turning to see what had caused the noise, our eyes were met by a truly frightening sight. Flying low in the sky was an aeroplane, smoke billowing from one of the engines on the wing.

It was coming straight for us!

'Get down!' I yelled, pushing Arthur to the ground and diving behind a garden wall.

A few seconds later, there was a tremendous roar as the plane hit the ground. Cautiously I raised my head above the wall and looked to where the plane had crashed. Arthur was also tentatively getting to his feet.

Two hundred yards ahead, a German bomber was burning furiously. Before we could fully get to our feet, there was a huge explosion as its ammunition detonated, generating an enormous fireball and a black mushroom cloud that rose high into the air, forcing us back to the ground. Despite being some distance away, the heat from the explosion was intense, forcing us both to turn away and shield our faces.

It was not lost on us just how close we had come to being killed. Being this close to death was not new to me, having nearly succumbed to diphtheria and been fished out of the North Sea by my sister as a youngster. It would have been a bit ironic to have then lost my life by being hit by a shot down German aeroplane.

From what I could see, as we observed the burning wreckage lighting up the evening sky, it looked like a Heinkel He-111. At the time I was not sure if it was that or a Junkers Ju-88.

I would become very familiar with both planes soon enough.

*   *   *

Once it became clear to the Nazi leadership they would not be able to defeat the RAF, they turned their attentions to Britain's major cities and ports. They commenced a massive bombing campaign with the intention of breaking the will of the British people to fight on, so forcing their leaders to sue for peace. This campaign became known to history simply as 'The Blitz'.

Commencing on 7 September 1940 and lasting until May the following year, London was attacked seventy-one times, with over 18,000 tons of bombs being dropped on the capital.

As a 16-year-old telegram boy working in the City, the Blitz was something I just had to endure with the rest of the population. The sound of air raid warning sirens and the sight of fires raging in the East End of London as the bombs, incendiaries and parachute mines wreaked havoc and destruction on the factories and warehouses of the docklands, became a daily and nightly occurrence. On many occasions I was forced to spend the night in the bomb shelters and tube stations near to where I worked, it being far too dangerous to head for home.

Without let up, in late 1940, for fifty-seven consecutive nights, searchlights scanned the skies between the rather ineffective barrage balloons, seeking out the Heinkels and Junkers of the Luftwaffe as they rained down their destructive cargoes upon the population. The night sky would be filled with the beams of searchlights and the sound of anti-aircraft guns as they fired their ack-ack, hoping to stop the enemy completing their missions. The East End suffered the most, taking a battering each night as the Germans targeted the industrial centres and docklands. It was obvious that the indiscriminate nature of the way the bombs fell meant the homes of the people who worked and lived in those places would also be hit. With thousands dead and injured, and many thousands more made homeless, people took shelter wherever they could: in cellars, public shelters and London Underground stations. And finally, on hearing the 'all clear', residents of the capital would emerge from their sanctuaries to find their houses and, on some occasions, their whole streets, obliterated by the Nazi bombs.

But London was not the only city under constant attack. Manchester, Birmingham and the port cities of Southampton and Liverpool were also under constant bombardment, their residents suffering like those in the capital.

Although under continual assault, the population would not be cowed into submission, and a general sense of 'we're all in this together' was felt throughout the country. I, too, believed the Germans could not break the will of the British people.

One eventful night during the Blitz, I found myself caught at work at Aldgate East Post Office. When the air-raid sirens wailed throughout the city, I realized I had no choice other than to join my colleagues taking shelter in the cellar. As we all huddled together, the sound of the bombs landing seemed very close, the building shaking above us as dust and plaster rained down on us from the ceiling above. The sound was almost deafening. We could hear anti-aircraft fire between the thud of the high explosive bombs and parachute mines, creating a cacophony of hellish proportions. On more than one occasion I feared for my life, as almighty explosions caused death and destruction on the streets above.

After a number of hours the bombing finally stopped and the high-pitched howl of the 'all clear' sounded. Slowly we got to our feet and dusted ourselves down, before cautiously going up the steps and out into the world once more.

What my colleagues and I witnessed now was the virtual demolition of the post office. It had taken a direct hit and was nothing more than a wreck, fires still burning in the building and the surrounding area. It was like a scene from the apocalypse, a vision of Dante's Hell. The devastation was total and heartbreaking. All around us fires burned, buildings stood in ruins and the cries of the injured wailed almost as loudly as the bombs themselves. Firefighters fought furiously to put out the fires and to rescue those trapped under the rubble. Oddly, many were to die from drowning and gassing as survivors were trapped in air pockets that quickly filled with water and gas from burst pipes.

How many had died in this raid, I could not be sure, but the total number of deaths throughout Britain during the Blitz was around 32,000, with another 87,000 seriously injured. The physical damage to the country was also enormous, with two million homes destroyed along with hundreds of warehouses and industrial units. The Blitz came to an end in May 1941, almost suddenly, when the German leadership, realizing they were getting nowhere in trying to defeat Britain this way, decided to concentrate their efforts elsewhere.

As the New Year arrived, I found myself on the move. My sister had relocated to the Post Office Savings Bank in Harrogate and so, at the age of seventeen, I decided to join her there. I, too, had managed to get a transfer, after first forging my father's signature giving permission.

I had grown very close to Annette during my teenage years. Although we had not been particularly close whilst living in Berwick, the move to Hornchurch had put the two of us in the same boat. Both of us had to settle in a new place where neither knew anyone, and so we leaned on each other for support in the early years after the move. This developed into a closeness that would last throughout our lives. However, Annette later had problems with our father, because he did not approve of her relationship with a young soldier, and so it was not long before she left home and moved in with her partner's parents.

Moving to Harrogate did not come without problems for me. During the day I worked at the Cairn Hydro Hotel, which had been commandeered by the GPO Contracts Department, and at night I stayed in digs in Johns Drive, Bilton, before moving to Strawberry Dale Terrace in the town centre. This did not come cheap and, as a young man on a very low income, I struggled. After all deductions were made from my wages and when I had paid for my accommodation, I was left with only five shillings a week to live on.

Desperate for a new pair of shoes, since the ones I wore were wearing thin due to all the walking I had to do, I wrote to my father in Hornchurch asking for assistance. After all, I was still technically a minor and my father was still legally responsible for me. A new pair of decent shoes would cost around thirty shillings, much more than I had saved. My father replied, telling me I had 'made my bed', and donated just ten shillings towards the shoes. Unhappy with his response, I immediately mailed the money back with a note to say that, obviously, it appeared he needed the money more than I did.

* * *

The slackening of the bombing raids on Britain coincided with one of the most eventful dates in the whole of the war, Sunday, 22 June 1941. The events of this day would have an indirect effect upon my life and that of many like me.

The Germans had been victorious throughout Europe, defeating every army that faced them. They occupied countries from Norway in the north-west to Greece in the south-east. Their armies of occupation numbered hundreds of thousands and they were a formidable enemy to anyone opposing them. As yet, only Britain and its Empire were still able to wage war against them, the English Channel proving Britain's saviour once more, as it had done throughout history. Unable to defeat Britain, Hitler now turned his attention to the east.

Hitler and Stalin had agreed a non-aggression pact in the summer of 1939, thus avoiding war between the Soviet Union and Germany. This meant Hitler was able to invade Poland unopposed and conduct war in the west without the fear of having to fight on two fronts. The pact was also beneficial to the Soviets, who were also able to 'take a slice' of the Polish pie; they had invaded the country from the east two weeks after the German invasion in the west. The Soviets also invaded Finland during the Winter War of 1939–1940, causing an unlikely alliance between Finland and the Nazis later in the war, as the Finns tried to retrieve the territories lost during that conflict.

'Operation Barbarossa', the invasion of the Soviet Union by Germany, came completely out of the blue. The Soviets were simply not expecting it. Unprepared and ill-equipped, they were not able to prevent very quick advances by the Nazis, and within a few days the Wehrmacht were deep inside Russian territory.

To Britain, the invasion of Russia by the Germans came as something of a relief. At last, we would not be fighting this war alone. Not long after the invasion, Stalin called to Churchill for help in halting the German advance. The Soviet Union needed vital supplies, in the form of tanks, aircraft, ammunition, food, medical supplies and various other war materiel, in order to effectively conduct a war against a superior force, both in numbers and in battle experience.

Churchill realized he had to give the Russians what they were asking for. Having an ally as potentially powerful as the Soviets could mean the war might yet be won. Hitler had made a massive mistake. The sheer number of people living in the Soviet Union would mean that given time and the right resources, they could produce a massive army, large enough to beat the Nazis and force them back. Without delay, Churchill ordered a convoy of war supplies to be sent to the ports of Murmansk and Archangel in the north-west of Russia, on the Barents and White Seas, and within two months of the invasion the first Arctic convoy set sail, via Iceland, for Russia.

*   *   *

I continued with my job at the GPO in Harrogate into the summer months, and as the second half of the year progressed I knew, since I would be eighteen years old in the coming December, that I would probably be called up soon to serve my country. With dreams of joining the Navy still very much alive within me, and not being put off by my failed attempt to join as a boy recruit a few years previously, I was determined that this branch was where I wanted to be.

And so, wishing to avoid a call up to the Army and inadvertently succumbing to my father's wishes, two weeks before my eighteenth birthday I walked into the Royal Navy recruiting office in Leeds and volunteered to join up. This time there was no brief interview in a dimly lit cellar, and I passed all the tests required (including the eye test, 20/20!). Being a volunteer I was able to pick the trade I wanted and opted for Seaman/Gunner. With a warrant to join the shore training base HMS *Ganges*, I set off for Suffolk on 5 December, the day after my eighteenth birthday, when I officially joined the Royal Navy, thereby achieving a dream I had had my whole life.

CHAPTER THREE

New Recruit

Now a fully fledged member of His Majesty's Royal Navy, I began my naval career, my initial basic training taking place at HMS *Ganges*.

Formerly a boys' training centre, in May 1940 HMS *Ganges* changed its operations to that of a 'Hostilities Only New Entry Training' establishment, specializing in training adult recruits for service on naval warships. Sited on the North Sea at Shotley, to the south of Ipswich and across the River Stour from Harwich, the shore base had been in existence since May 1865. It was a large unit with many facilities that gave excellent training to equip recruits with the necessary skills for their upcoming service on warships.

As well as many shore-based amenities, which included sports fields, a fully equipped gymnasium, barrack rooms and mess facilities, the *Ganges* also had many sailing craft in which the recruits could hone their skills on the waters of the Stour, the River Orwell and the North Sea.

Despite being a new recruit, I felt I had something of an advantage over many of my new comrades. My abilities as a gymnast whilst at school, coupled with the parade ground training I had received as part of 'Max Karo's Army' meant I felt a confidence higher than many of my friends. It was clear to the instructors I was a capable individual, and I would often help out others in getting to grips with the specifics of parade ground drill. My training by the Guards meant I was sometimes singled out to demonstrate to the other recruits how certain drills should be done. But this confidence in me was no perk; it being winter, the parade ground occasionally had six inches of snow lying upon it.

However, Navy life suited me. It was all I had hoped it would be. My enthusiasm to learn new skills made me a favourite with the instructors, and I was very keen on getting to a ship and putting those skills to use. The three months spent at the *Ganges* went by all too quickly, and once I had passed out I was drafted to

St Mary's Barracks in Chatham to complete a gunnery course. Learning how to set fuses, load and fire the massive 4.7 inch naval guns, along with other weapons, and utilizing the 'yaw, pitch and roll' simulator, recruits were taught how to range, aim and fire the various naval weaponry we might need to use once on board a ship. In a slightly more relaxed atmosphere here than at the *Ganges*, I found the training exciting, and once it was completed, I was pleased to learn I was to be posted to a brand new destroyer, HMS *Milne*, as an Ordinary Seaman Gunlayer (Third Class).

At that time HMS *Milne*, an 'M' class destroyer, was conducting trials in Scotland in preparation for service as Flotilla Leader in the 3rd Destroyer Flotilla as part of the Home Fleet. Work had commenced on the ship in January 1940 at Scott's Shipbuilders of Greenock, and she was launched in December 1941. Work continued on the ship and trials took place in July and August, until she eventually joined the 3rd Flotilla in September 1942.

My posting to the *Milne* occurred during the trial phase, and I was ordered to report to John Brown's Yard in Clydebank as part of the advance party. The ship had been towed there from Greenock due to bomb damage at the shipyard. As she was yet to be commissioned, I was billeted in digs on shore, a private house owned by a Mrs Mackintosh, with a shipmate, a man in his forties who had been recalled to service as a reservist.

My companion was married with a family; he was not too enamoured of his forced return to the Navy, and he let it show. After all, he had served his country already, he complained, albeit during peacetime, but service is service at the end of the day. That being said, he was able to offer me, who was less than half his age, the benefit of his experience in how best to adapt to life on board ship.

Seeing the *Milne* for the first time took my breath away. With an overall length of 362ft and a beam of 37ft, she was an impressive sight. Parsons geared steam turbines, each driving one propeller shaft, gave her a total of 48,000 horsepower and an impressive maximum speed of 37 knots. Her range, at a steady fifteen knots, was 5,500 miles. Painted in the destroyer's colours of green and white camouflage, she had the fleet number G14 emblazoned on her side.

Equipped as a flotilla leader, the ship's firepower consisted of six 4.7 inch Mark XI guns in twin-gun-mounted turrets, housed in front of the bridge and also behind the superstructure, one of which I would be operating as a seaman gunner. She was also fitted with a quadruple mount for above-water torpedoes and with two depth charge throwers and racks containing forty-two depth charges. For defence against air attack the ship had a QF 4-inch Mark V anti-aircraft gun, a QF two pounder 'pom-pom' gun, two Oerlikon 20mm cannons and four 0.5 inch Vickers Mark III anti-aircraft guns. In all, she was a heavily armed vessel and should have no problem in defending herself.

As we approached the ship for the first time we were stopped at the gangplank by a Petty Officer holding a clipboard. He looked at us indifferently and after a few words of explanation advised us the ship was not quite ready for us and there was nothing for us to do. He sent us both away with instructions to return the following day.

As we walked away, my roommate was not best pleased. In fact he was downright annoyed. He moaned that he had already done twelve years in the Navy and had left his wife and children after being ordered to return to the mob. Now that he was here, in the middle of nowhere, he was being told his services were not yet required. He would have stayed at home had he known this was going to happen.

I told him I was sure we would be needed soon enough and maybe we should make the best of the time off we had been granted. After all, we both knew it probably would not last long.

Each day, the two of us reported to the ship as requested, and for the first three weeks we simply spent an hour or so on board before being told to go home and await further orders, which never came. This gave me a chance to explore the area and have some fun. It was not long before my charms had won the favours of a local girl, Mary, who worked at the biscuit factory close by, and we spent many afternoons strolling along the river and surrounding area, chatting and holding hands. Unfortunately, she had a very strict father, who did not approve of her mixing with 'rough sailors', and consequently I was never able to take her to a dance.

Eventually, my roommate and I were called upon to join the rest of the crew for sea trials, and so I finally got to stay on board.

The ship had a crew of 224, and the majority of us, almost eighty per cent, were new to the Navy, this being our first posting. The remainder of the crew was made up of experienced sailors, and it was these who would show the ropes to us new lads.

The ship's captain, Captain Ian Murray Robertson Campbell, addressed the crew once all were on board. It was a short speech, concise and to the point, emphasizing teamwork, efficiency and comradeship. 'A happy ship is an efficient ship', he declared, and the crew were thus inspired to work hard for him and show just how efficient and capable we could be.

My action station was as turret trainer on 'B' turret, located to the front of the bridge. This was an enclosed turret which had a Petty Officer in charge directing operations. The turret housed twin 4.7 inch guns, and I spent many days going through weapons drills, as well as carrying out other responsibilities which included mess duties. With sixteen men to a mess, the sailors took turns in preparing the meals and organizing the mess budget. Some, of course, were better at it than others, providing good nourishing food, whereas the skills of the less able left a lot to be desired. Each of us took turns in preparing the meals and taking the ingredients to the galley for cooking. I soon found I had a certain amount of skill in making short pastry, but others had no aptitude whatsoever.

When not on active service, the men were able to sling and sleep in their hammocks. I found a good spot, attaching my hammock between two stanchions above an electric fire. However, we new sailors had to quickly become heavy sleepers, as our shipmates would not be quiet, often playing cards and chatting directly below anyone trying to get some rest.

During mid-August, in preparation for active service, HMS *Milne* carried out a number of anti-submarine exercises with the short-range escort destroyer HMS *Windsor*, the Norwegian destroyer HNoMS *Eskdale*, the Greek destroyer RHS *Kanaris* and a Royal Navy submarine, HMS *Upright*. This kept the new crew on our toes and helped us all to settle in to our new roles.

As the ship had not yet been commissioned for service, the Admiralty and Ministry of Information gave permission for her to assist in the making of a new film.

'In Which We Serve' was to be a patriotic movie inspired by the exploits of Lord Louis Mountbatten and the sinking of his ship, HMS *Kelly*, during the Battle of Crete. The film was written and directed by Noel Coward. Coward himself starred as the ship's captain, along with many other notable actors of the time, including Richard Attenborough, John Mills, Bernard Miles and Celia Johnson. The film unit spent some time on board taking shots of the crew, who had to dress in tropical gear to simulate a ship off the coast of Gibraltar, as opposed to its actual location near to the Isle of Arran. A lot of the footage of HMS *Milne* was used in the finished film, which went on to be a success at the box office.

CHAPTER FOUR

Settling In

Whilst I was settling into the Navy in Scotland, enjoying the relative peace with my new shipmates, the Royal Navy was carrying out operations in many theatres of war. One such was the convoy route to Russia, otherwise known as the Arctic convoy, or to the men who sailed it, the 'Kola Run'.

With remarkable speed, the first convoy of supplies to our new allies set sail a mere two months after the Nazi invasion of Russia. This was an amazing logistical feat considering the amount of supplies and the number of ships that needed to be organized.

The mustering points for the convoys were initially in Iceland, at Faxa Bay, Reykjavik and Hvalfjödur, before moving south to Loch Ewe in north-west Scotland in 1942. From these assembly points the ships sailed eastward towards Norway and then onward to Russia to deliver their cargoes. The route took them along the Norwegian coast and then around the northern tip of Scandinavia before heading east to the ports of Murmansk on the Barents Sea, just inside the Kola Inlet, and to Archangel, further east on the White Sea. The route varied according to the season, the frozen pack ice in wintertime making it impossible to sail too far north.

These routes to Russia were hazardous for many reasons. Firstly, the weather. The harshness of the climate in that region of the world can never be underestimated. Savage storms would appear from nowhere, creating waves 50ft and 60ft high, violently throwing around any vessel attempting to sail through them. The cold of the Arctic the further north the ships sailed caused havoc with equipment and men alike. Sailors had to step out on to frozen decks to clear ice and snow for fear of their ship becoming top-heavy and capsizing. Many ships were lost in this way, and should any unfortunate soul fall into the sea, they had at most two minutes to get out of the water before they froze to death. Temperatures as low as minus 30º centigrade, ten degrees lower than a modern household freezer, meant that being outside for too long was extremely hazardous. Added to this was the wind-chill factor, which made it feel much, much colder.

As well as having to contend with the highly inclement weather, the convoys also had to endure the constant threat of U-boat attack. Operating in 'wolf packs', Nazi submarines trailed the convoys, picking off ships wherever possible. Despite the advent of Asdic (sonar), and each convoy having dedicated anti-submarine ships escorting them, many ships fell to their torpedoes; thousands of tons of shipping and many lives, military and merchant, were lost in the process.

Surface ships also posed a considerable threat, with the battleships *Scharnhorst* and *Tirpitz* operating out of the Norwegian fjords. Should they manage to locate a convoy and conduct a co-ordinated attack, they were liable to cause massive damage. However, Hitler was extremely cautious in using the surface ships of the Kriegsmarine to any considerable degree, for fear of losing them and of the effect any such loss could have on German morale. It seems strange that despite having such mighty weapons at his disposal, ships that could have done untold damage to the convoys, they were never really used as they could have been throughout the war.

Finally, and the most persistently hazardous of all, there was the Luftwaffe. As the convoys got closer to the Norwegian coastline, they fell prey to air attack from the Nazis' northern bases. It became a common thing to see wave after wave of He-111s and Ju-88s attacking the convoys with torpedoes and bombs, sinking many merchant and Royal Navy ships. Air attacks were most prevalent in the summer months, when the days were longer and flying was less hazardous for the pilots. However, the time spent under air attack was also less in the summer, since the convoys were able to sail further north, away from the air bases, leaving the enemy planes with less time to carry out their attacks. During the winter months, with the weather being worse and daylight only a few hours long, the opportunity for air attack was diminished. However, the convoys had to sail closer to the coastline to avoid icebergs and floes and so came well within range of the Nazi bombers.

Either way you looked at it, no matter the time of year, there was always one hazard or another, with the underwater threat being something of a constant.

Each convoy was allocated a code number. In the initial stages of the Arctic convoys these began with 'PQ', followed by a sequential number for the outward journey to Russia, and then 'QP' for the return leg. The initials came from an operations officer at the Admiralty, Commander Phillip Quellyn-Roberts, later changing to JW for the outbound journey and RA for the return. The convoys contained, on average, around fifty ships in total, and set out in columns 1,000 yards apart. Each ship in the column was positioned 500 yards astern of the ship in front and was allocated a pennant number. So, for example, a pennant number of 24 signified the fourth ship in the second column.

Despite the top speed of some of the escorting ships being over 30 knots, the convoy sailed at the speed of its slowest member, an average of around 8 knots, which made the merchant ships easy prey for a good Luftwaffe pilot with a couple of torpedoes. Due to this slow speed, the convoys took an average of eight days to get from Reykjavik to Murmansk and a further two to reach Archangel. However, enemy attacks and avoiding ice floes could add days on to each trip.

*   *   *

When, in September 1942, HMS *Milne* was commissioned for service, me and my pals' hopes of a voyage somewhere warm and sunny were quickly dashed. A tour of the Mediterranean, despite all the dangers of that particular area of operations, was clearly preferable to the storms and dangers of the Atlantic run or the Russian convoys. However, no sooner had the ship been deemed fit for active service than Captain Campbell received orders to take her to Scapa Flow to join the Third Destroyer Flotilla in the Home Fleet. Orders were then received to provide part of the fighting escort for convoy number PQ18. This was not altogether unexpected as the ship had been painted in the colours of the Arctic, white and green.

This caused a little nervousness on board ship. News had by now reached us of the debacle of the previous convoy, PQ17.

PQ17 had set out on 27 June, heading for Archangel. As the convoy closed on Norway, information from Allied agents arrived at the Admiralty stating that the German 'Bismarck'-class battleship *Tirpitz* had left her base near Trondheim and was headed for waters which the convoy was approaching. Although this information in the end proved to be incorrect, it did not prevent panic erupting in the Admiralty, and the infamous order was sent to the convoy, by Admiral Sir Dudley Pound, for the ships to 'scatter' and the covering force to be withdrawn. To scatter meant the ships were to head off in any and all directions in an attempt to stop the enemy from destroying them all. This effectively left the merchant ships unprotected, and over the next few days, twenty-four of the thirty-five merchantmen that had headed out from Iceland were sunk, with the loss of over 150 lives. It was a disaster.

*   *   *

After what had happened to PQ17, the crew of the *Milne* were not exactly thrilled to be going on the Kola Run.

Sitting in the mess deck, we mulled over the news. There was a certain amount of trepidation at the thought of setting off on the same journey that had ended in abject failure only a few weeks previously, but we all knew what we'd signed up for. If the Admiralty had decided another convoy was necessary, then we would just have to get on with it. There was no point worrying about it.

As I sipped at my kye (a sort of hot chocolate drink), we discussed how the Navy might now be approaching the upcoming journey. It was clear to us they would do everything they could to prevent the disaster of PQ17 from happening again, and they were more than likely to ensure the escort for the convoy had sufficient firepower to repel any attack. We were sure we would be given the necessary resources to ensure a successful voyage.

As far as the personal issue of uniform was concerned, this was certainly true. We sailors had been supplied with a lot of good cold-weather gear. This included padded, hooded duffel coats that were lined with lambswool and had an extra hood with slits for the eyes and mouth. We had also been given underwear so thick you could have turned it into a sweater, and as a gunner I was issued with a knee-length sheepskin jerkin. We were also provided with mittens with a separate thumb and index finger, along with scarves, helmet liners and balaclavas.

Some sailors were not too sure why we were aiding the Russians in this way, risking our lives to get supplies to them. They were unsure whether our new allies deserved it. There was a feeling amongst some of 'Why should we help them, when they left us to it when we needed them?' They argued the Russians were only in the war due to being invaded and had left Britain to fight alone up until that time. I could see their point, but there was nothing any of us sailors could do about that. If the Navy said we were going to Russia, then it was to Russia we would go.

I was aware the Russian convoys had commenced only two months after the Germans had invaded the Soviet Union and, at the time, was not sure if this was more a political thing than an effective military strategy. Whereas the Americans had provided practical help, by means of loaning military equipment under the 'Lend-Lease' agreement, the Russians had done nothing to assist Britain in her hour of need. To others, as well as to my good friend, Charlie 'Robbo' Robinson, this did not sit quite right.

However, the politics of it all was not something the men would dwell on for too long, our thoughts turning more to the logistics of the upcoming journey and how it would affect us. We knew we just had to ensure we all did the jobs we had been trained to do, to the best of our ability. I was confident I would be able to do my bit when the time came. Although there was a new nervousness about the ship, I could sense that as well as a slight sense of anxiety amongst some of the crew, there was also a new sense of purpose. The trials were now complete, the ship was ready and the war was waiting. And for everyone on board, as far as I could see, there was now a real sense of 'let's get this thing done'. I looked at my friend Robbo across the table as he tucked into a plate of spam fritters and smiled. As the captain had stated in his opening address, an efficient ship was a happy ship, and I was very much of the opinion HMS *Milne* was indeed that, a happy ship.

CHAPTER FIVE

PQ18, the Kola Run

Reykjavik, Iceland – 9 September 1942

From the shelter of 'B' turret, I looked out across the water. To the left, and for as far as I could see in the fading light, columns of ships stretched to the horizon. Merchant vessels with the flags of Great Britain, USA, the Soviet Union and Panama, each loaded with vital supplies for the fighting men of Russia. All protected by a formidable naval force comprising many ships. HMS *Milne* had been ordered to rendezvous here and then support and protect the convoy as it sailed to Murmansk in northern Russia. Some of the ships would then continue on to Archangel on the White Sea.

There was no denying that, like my shipmates, I felt a sense of nervous apprehension about the whole thing. Up until now, we had merely been in a sort of 'training' mode and had not been in any real danger. However, things were now different. This was all very real. The increase in tension aboard ship was tangible; the guns had been tested, cleared and tested again, and exercises carried out ensuring all the ship's company knew exactly what we needed to do should 'action stations' be called. When on deck all eyes scanned the sea edgily, looking for any break in the water that would give away a periscope, or the track of a torpedo from a U-boat that had somehow managed to get close enough to fire at us. And although we knew we were out of range of any enemy airfield, some of us also looked to the sky, worried a Junkers or Heinkel might swoop down at any moment to unload its torpedoes and bombs upon an unsuspecting crew.

As I looked at the assembled craft that had set sail from Loch Ewe a week ago, I understood the escort ships were not the main target of the Nazis. It was those merchant ships carrying the supplies they were mostly after. To me, they looked too small and ill-equipped to defend themselves, some having almost no means of protection whatsoever, whilst others merely had a couple of twin Browning machine guns with which to repel any attack. My respect went out to all who sailed on them. They were civilians after all, and the crews were very small. The peacetime sailors of the merchant ships relied totally upon the escorts of the Royal Navy for their very survival. And so many had been sunk already in this war.

I pulled my woollen hat over my ears and scratched at my stubbled face. I had not yet had a chance to shave and knew I might not get one. Captain Campbell had put the whole ship on full alert. The convoy was about to set course on the most perilous stage of the voyage. It was heading for the waters where the previous convoy, PQ17, had met its unfortunate fate.

This time, though, I was sure things would be different.

The Admiralty had waited over nine weeks after PQ17 before sending out another convoy. PQ18 was to have a fighting escort consisting of sixteen destroyers, the *Milne* being one of them. It was also supported by a close escort group made up of various corvettes, minesweepers, anti-submarine and anti-aircraft ships. The flagship, the light cruiser HMS *Scylla* in which the commander, Rear Admiral Bob Burnett, sailed, headed the whole convoy. What made this convoy unique was that it was the first to include an aircraft carrier, the converted cargo ship HMS *Avenger*, which carried three Swordfish reconnaissance aircraft and twelve Sea Hurricanes.

I truly felt for the pilots of the Hurricanes. Once they were catapulted into the air they had no way of landing back on board as the flight deck was too short. Once they were out of ammunition or fuel, or their operations were complete, they would have to ditch their aircraft in the sea as close to the rescue ship, SS *Copeland*, as they could, and await rescue before they froze to death. Their survival would depend on how quickly they could be pulled out of the water. The *Milne* crew had been warned about just how cold these waters were; to end up in the sea this far north would mean certain death if you were not recovered in quick time. I shivered as I thought about it.

Seeing me shiver, the Petty Officer supervising 'B' turret laughed. 'You think this is cold?' he said. 'Wait until you get to the Barents. Now, *that's* cold!'

I thought back to the previous few days. We had set sail from Scapa Flow on 3 September with orders to join the convoy in Iceland. The date was not lost on me, it being the third anniversary of the outbreak of war. I thought back to what I had been doing then, delivering telegrams in the City of London for the GPO. How far I had come in those three years!

At one point on the voyage to Iceland, Captain Campbell invited a few of us to the bridge to take turns at the wheel. This was the first time I had managed to get a good look at the man. Tall, handsome and impeccably dressed, he set a good example of how a ship's captain should look. Well-mannered and amiable, he put us young sailors at ease and even conducted a little small talk, asking after our families and how we were liking life in the Navy.

When it came to my turn to take the wheel, I had never felt so important in all my life. Here I was, a young lad from Berwick, now in charge of a Royal Navy warship, turning the wheel to the captain's orders. I smiled to myself. I had come so far. Not long ago I was delivering telegrams among the ruins of London, now I was guiding a ship towards Iceland to fight those Nazis that had laid the capital to waste. It was not very often I felt proud of myself, but this was certainly a time to feel a real sense of achievement.

As we got closer to Iceland, the lookouts were doubled and the guns were permanently manned. U-Boat 'wolf packs' had operated in these areas, and the crew hoped the Asdic operators in the Electronic Warfare Operations (EWO) room were alert to their screens. They would be the first to spot any sign of enemy activity, be it from sea or air.

Standing on the deck and looking at the land as it gradually came closer, I felt a tap on my shoulder and turned to look. It was my friend Robbo, who handed me a cup. I was pleased to see it was kye, the steam rising into the air and mixing with the steam of my breath as I blew on the top of the cup.

Remarking how cold it was, he joked that I might have wished I'd joined the Army, just as my father had suggested.

I smiled at him and replied, 'No. I wouldn't miss this for anything.'

We were then ordered back to our positions by the Petty Officer. I quickly swallowed some more of the warm liquid and made to comply with the order.

There was movement to my left and I looked to the side. A sailor had moved to the gunwale and, finding a break in the rails, unzipped his fly and urinated over the side of the ship. I smiled to myself. Often my mates would be caught short like this, having to make their way to their duty stations without first going to the toilet. Not able to leave their posts, they would shuffle off to answer the call of nature only a few feet from their duty station. The officers, not wishing to make a fuss, tended to let it go.

Now we were on a war footing, the watches had become more frequent. Instead of four hours on duty followed by eight hours off, our downtime, (which was never really leisure on a fighting ship) was now cut in half, meaning there was only four hours between duties. When not at our duty locations we were expected to eat, shower, carry out any other tasks our Petty Officers and Chief Petty Officers might need us to, and also get some sleep. Like most on board, I had become a heavy sleeper. I was able to lie down almost anywhere and sleep undisturbed, despite the hubbub and noise around me. Setting up hammocks had been stopped once we were at sea. We had been told they would come in useful to plug any gaps should the ship be hit, and so the crew just slept wherever we could comfortably lay our heads. It was a case of having to make do.

It was evening and I looked to the west, where a fiery sunset greeted my eyes. The ships had now formed up in their respective columns and, once morning came and the *Scylla* had taken her position tucked in behind the front screen, the aircraft carrier HMS *Avenger* astern of her, we set sail, pushing out from the island into the open sea, heading north-east in the direction of northern Norway and towards our ultimate destination. HMS *Milne* was positioned at the front of the convoy, on the starboard side.

Once more at my position in 'B' turret, I knew now things were very real. We were heading out to war.

*   *   *

It was not long before 'action stations' sounded. Lying in the mess deck, fully clothed and with my life jacket inflated (to provide more comfort), I jumped to my feet as the sirens wailed over the tannoy system and all around the ship. Fully appreciating this was no drill, my shipmates and I ran as fast as we could to our duty areas. I arrived only seconds later at 'B' turret to man the training gear of the 4.7 inch QF guns. This was something I had spent many hours at HMS *Ganges* and the gunnery school at Chatham training for, and I was pleased it all came naturally to me.

It was 9 September and we were only a few miles out of Iceland, travelling at an approximate speed of 9 knots, not quite yet within range of the Luftwaffe stations based in Norway. Word got around that U-boats may have been sighted, and when I looked to the rear of the convoy I could see a Swordfish biplane in the air, the pilot and spotter on the lookout for any telltale signs of enemy activity. Even from this distance I could clearly see the long torpedo suspended underneath its fuselage. If the German submariners knew a plane was in the air on the lookout for them, they would dive immediately. Although the Swordfish crew might be unsuccessful in finding them, the enemy would at least be scared off from trying to attack the convoy.

The Petty Officer seemed unconcerned. He was an experienced sailor who had been on many convoys. He explained the U-boats would probably not attack yet, but would be forming into packs ahead of us, lying in wait.

There was a nervous murmur as the rest of the gun crew thought about what he had told us, but we did not say anything. We understood he was an experienced seaman and knew what he was talking about.

As the day wore on, we were put through our paces, checking and cleaning weapons ready for the fight we knew was to come. Torpedo tubes' crews went purposefully about their work, cleaning and preparing the torpedoes ready for instant use, should they be required. Those in the gun turrets and the men manning the Oerlikons and Bofors checked, re-checked and then checked again the workings of the weapons that the life of the ship depended on.

The following day, word got round that the four British submarines patrolling the Norwegian coast had spotted the German ships *Scheer*, *Hipper* and *Köln*. It was now becoming apparent that the German success against the ill-fated PQ17 had given them a renewed confidence that they could smash the Arctic convoy route once and for all. Another disaster would necessitate a complete rethink on the part of the British Admiralty and a probable ending of the support Britain was giving our Russian allies. It was therefore essential PQ18 was a success, not just in getting the cargoes to the Russian ports, but also in defeating a confident and capable enemy.

The next day, 11 September, with no further sighting of enemy activity, Admiral Burnett in the *Scylla* signalled the 3rd Flotilla to join him in heading to Spitzbergen to refuel. The 3rd Flotilla formed part of 'Force B', leaving 'Force A' to take fuel from the escorting tankers and continue on with the convoy to provide protection whilst we were away. 'Force B', once refuelled, would then head at full steam to rejoin the convoy as it entered more dangerous waters.

The Spitzbergen coastline was a welcome sight to the crew on the *Milne*, and as the ships entered Lowe Sound we looked in wonder at the ice-covered terrain and the dark mass of a glacier, parts of which had broken off, falling into the water to become icebergs. The sun's rays bouncing off them gave them a jewel-like appearance. There looked to be no signs of life on land, but for a fleeting second I thought I saw movement high up on a snowy ridge. I scanned the horizon seeking out the thing that had caught my eye. I was not sure what it could have been, but the Petty Officer suggested it might have been a polar bear; they were not uncommon and had been known to venture this far south.

A row of oil tankers lined the Sound, and as each ship docked to their sides to take on heated fuel, there was bustling activity on the decks of the destroyers. Along with the *Scylla* that had led us into the Sound, ahead were three other 'M' class destroyers, HMS *Marne*, HMS *Martin* and HMS *Meteor*. As the ships passed, the crews waved to each other in greeting. There may have been a rivalry between the ships' companies whilst in port, but out here in the frozen wastes of the Arctic we had a mutual respect.

By morning the ships were once again full of fuel and ready to return to the convoy. Following the *Scylla*, the destroyers headed at full speed to rejoin them. Above us the clouds were low, and it was not long before a fog hit the ships. It was not to last long and as it cleared there was a noticeable speck in the air some distance away.

'Junkers 88, I think,' stated the Petty Officer, his binoculars clamped to his eyes. 'Probably an observation aircraft out looking for us. Expect some action any time soon, boys.'

On hearing these words, I could feel my heart thumping inside my chest.

Without warning, the 'action stations' sounded around the ship, and I could hear it being taken up by the other ships further out to sea. The unmistakable drone of aircraft engines could be heard off the starboard bow and suddenly, emerging through a break in the clouds, an He-111 appeared. I recognized it instantly and was taken back to that night in Hornchurch in 1940, when one had nearly crashed on top of me.

Immediately the pom-poms and Oerlikons opened up, firing their ordnance in the direction of the approaching aircraft and, as if caught by surprise, the pilot turned the plane away, putting a safe distance between himself and the ships below. After a while the Heinkel faded from view and was gone.

This was the first time the *Milne*'s guns had been fired in anger, and a sense of exhilaration permeated the crew. We had been called upon to protect the ship and we had done it perfectly.

That same afternoon, the convoy was spotted, and once again the destroyers took up our positions, bringing the escort back up to full strength. My crewmates and I looked again in awe at the sight before us: seventeen destroyers and eleven smaller warships, together with three anti-aircraft ships and an aircraft carrier to support and protect the merchant vessels. We were a formidable armada in anyone's book.

Word got round that the previous evening, while we were being refuelled in Spitzbergen, the convoy had been involved in an action. Patrolling Swordfish aircraft had spotted a U-boat 'wolf pack' closing in and had managed to scare most of them away. However, one of them (which turned out to be *U88*) had waited patiently ahead of the convoy, diving deep to allow the escort screen to pass over it. Unbeknown to the U-boat commander, he had been picked up by the Asdic operators on HMS *Faulknor*, commanded by Captain Alan Scott-Moncrieff. As the *Faulknor* sailed over the submarine, the British destroyer released a number of depth charges. It soon became clear, from the debris that surfaced following the explosions, that she had scored a direct hit and the *U88* was done for.

However, any sense of elation at having sunk the submarine was countered with the knowledge that a large number of mariners had died beneath the icy seas. But then, this was a case of kill or be killed. The U-boat commander would have had no hesitation in firing a torpedo into the side of any craft that came within his sights, consigning those on board to a watery grave.

*   *   *

The U-boats were nothing if not persistent. Throughout the following day, 13 September 1942, Swordfish from the *Avenger* flew numerous missions to keep the 'wolf pack' at bay. No sooner had the planes spotted a submarine than, seeing the danger, it would dive below the surface and away. The top speed of a submerged U-boat was a mere 4 knots, half the speed of the slowest ship of the convoy, and so, with all of them forced beneath the waves, the convoy was able to speed ahead. However, once some distance had been gained and the air was clear of British aircraft, the U-boats would resurface and follow on at 10 knots, slowly gaining on the surface ships to harry them once more. The range of a U-boat was significantly reduced by constant submerging, so they had to remain on the surface as much as possible.

Unfortunately, in the morning, the convoy suffered its first casualties. The U-boat *U408*, sensing an opportunity, fired three torpedoes in the direction of the Soviet cargo ship *Stalingrad*, carrying a consignment of munitions. One of the torpedoes hit home, rupturing her boiler and forcing the crew to abandon ship. Turning hard to port to avoid hitting the stricken ship, the American Liberty vessel SS *Oliver Ellsworth* was struck by another of the torpedoes, and she, too, had to be abandoned. Survivors were then picked up by the rescue ship *Copeland* and HMS *St Kenan*. The latter scuttled the drifting *Oliver Ellsworth*, firing a number of shells into her side after all the survivors had been rescued. In all, out of a combined crew of 158, 22 mariners lost their lives.

If a wake-up call was needed to those of us on the other ships, this was it.

Now on constant alert, I and the others in 'B' turret scanned the horizon for any signs of danger. We were told by the Petty Officer to stay alert and to keep ourselves warm, for we needed to be ready to act at a moment's notice.

I took the man's advice and beat my arms around my chest. The temperature was by now well below freezing, and although I was well wrapped up in the good Arctic clothing the Navy had provided, the cold was still penetrating through. It was bitterly cold, worse than anything I remembered as a child in Berwick. I was just glad I had the shelter of the turret to shield me from some of the worst of it, and felt for those poor lads manning the Oerlikons and Bofors who were more open to the elements.

Due to the sinking of the two merchant ships, there was now a clear gap in the starboard column, so the destroyers manoeuvred themselves to adjust their screening stations to compensate.

We could then hear the distant throbbing sound of Ju-88 air-craft as they looked for gaps in the clouds to come down and attack us. We were told to prepare ourselves and immediately returned to our stations.

I settled myself at the training gear handles to the right of the gun, ready to wind them as directed, to rotate the turret on the central pivot to position it for firing. My crewmate sitting to my side, known as the Layer, took hold of the elevator gear handles, his job being to raise the barrels. In the middle stood four more men, the loaders, all set to pump the shells into the breech as they were delivered by the shell hoist from the maga-zine below deck. All this was overseen by the calm, experienced Petty Officer standing behind us who would take instruction from the gunnery officer and fire control officer in the director, above the bridge.

From my position I became aware of activity on the air-craft carrier *Avenger*. Five Sea Hurricanes hurriedly took to the skies. There then followed a period in which the British planes hounded the attacking Junkers as, finding the occasional break in the clouds, they emerged to drop their bombs.

Working the huge weapon purposefully, us gunners in 'B' turret joined in with the other guns of the ships and fired our shells skyward. The 'boom! boom!' of the guns resounded in our ears as the ordnance flew from the twin barrels at a velocity of over 2,500ft per second, to explode high in the sky. The loaders methodically put the 62lb shells into the breech, at a rate of ten rounds a minute. Despite the bitter cold, a mix of hard work and adrenalin caused us to break into a sweat.

Oddly, I felt no fear, and I am sure it was the same for my comrades. The training we had received at HMS *Ganges* and Chatham now fully kicked in. It had prepared us all well for this, our first combat.

Among the noise of the anti-aircraft guns from the escort ships, we could hear the German bombs landing amongst the convoy and exploding just below the surface of the sea, the concussion throwing seawater high into the sky.

After only a few minutes the order was given to cease fire. Breaking my concentration, I looked to the sky and could see that the German planes were retreating, heading back to their Norwegian bases.

'They've wasted their time,' said the PO, now standing just outside the turret with his binoculars at his eyes. 'They've missed every ship . . . Well done, lads. Great work.'

We were convinced the Germans would think twice before they came back again. We had put up a formidable barrage, and anyone attempting to fly through it would have needed to be highly skilled and also very brave. However, the Petty Officer dispelled our optimism immediately. He told us we could count on them returning and, now they knew what firepower we had, they would be back in more significant numbers. He told us to stay alert and be ready when it happened.

I stood up to stretch my legs. The brief skirmish with the Luftwaffe had been tiring physically, but mentally even more so. This was the first action I had been involved in, and the pressure to make sure I carried out the instructions of my superiors and applied all I had been taught and practised over the past few months had weighed heavy. But overall, I was pleased with my performance. When called upon to do my bit I had done it without hesitation and to a standard that could not be bettered.

There was movement to my left and I saw it was my friend Robbo. Taking his cigarettes from his pocket he placed one in his mouth, then took off his mitten and lit it. We chatted for a few minutes as we watched the ships push forward, their wakes cutting deep grooves into the surface of the sea as we powered ahead, away from our attackers and towards our ultimate destination of the Kola Inlet. Now the German aircraft had gone, a sense of calm seemed to descend over the ship, although everyone was still at a heightened sense of alert.

Thirty minutes passed, the time being used to again check the guns and ensure they were ready for action should they be called upon to defend the convoy once more.

We did not have to wait long. A message came over the t noy that forty-four enemy aircraft were heading our way. Rol took my telescope and pointed it out to the southern horizon.

'They're not planes,' he said. 'They're birds. I wonder wl species they are.'

I looked in the direction he was indicating. A flock what look like dark birds, spreading out across the sky, no more th 200ft above the sea's surface, were headed in our direction.

'Those aren't birds,' said the PO. 'They're Heinkels . . . ar Junkers.'

'No, PO,' replied Robbo, shaking his head. 'They're birds, the are. I'm sure of it.'

'Trust me,' replied the PO. 'That's the Luftwaffe. There lool around fifty of them . . . And each of those planes will hav two torpedoes strapped to them. Get to your stations, lads.'

I wasn't prepared to debate the issue and quickly got myse back into position at the training gear just as 'action station once again sounded throughout the ship.

I took a breath. I was ready.

If the Germans wanted a fight, then I was going to giv them one.

CHAPTER SIX

Under Attack

They came in low and fast. Seeking out targets for their torpedoes.

As they loomed closer, the destroyers and anti-aircraft ships of the escort turned to meet them, our guns spitting fire at the low-flying aircraft, flak exploding in deadly bursts, spraying shrapnel all around them. It appeared the Germans were going all out, throwing as many Ju-88s and He-111s into the attack as they could muster.

There was no doubt that after PQ17 the enemy's confidence was sky high, and it showed in the way their pilots were flying. If they could hammer this new convoy then they might be able to stop the supply of war materiel to Russia once and for all. As far as the Allies were concerned, it was imperative PQ18 was a complete success. Another disaster could not be contemplated.

I spun the handles purposefully, turning the turret as quickly as I could toward the approaching German squadrons. Whether the 4.7 inch guns could be effective against low-flying aircraft was debatable, the barrels not able to fire on too low a trajectory, but I could hear the Oerlikons and Bofors also spewing out their ordnance, along with the other ships in the screen.

It appeared the release of the five Sea Hurricanes earlier may have been a little premature, now that the main force was attacking in such numbers. They were too few to have much effect in repelling the attackers. It was now up to the destroyers of the fleet to stop them.

In 'B' turret we worked furiously to get the German planes in our sights, the Petty Officer barking out orders, liaising with the fire control team above the bridge. He also offered words of encouragement to us young men, the majority of whom, myself included, were virtually new recruits.

Amongst the noise of the turret guns, I could hear the planes shooting close by and the sound of vicious explosions outside. I could not be certain what they were and decided not to think about it. I had no control over what was happening on the other ships. I knew I just had to carry out my duty efficiently and hope that what I was doing, along with all the other crews on the warships, would be enough to protect the lightly armed merchantmen. As I adjusted the turret, following the ever-changing pointer as the target area was amended by the gunnery officer, I did not have time to worry about what was happening around me. However, I was fully aware of my mates loading and firing the guns at a very fast rate. The noise was constant, but I had to maintain my concentration throughout the attack. It was both physically and mentally demanding, particularly when my shipmates and I were already very tired due to lack of sleep.

Outside, the battle was becoming ferocious. Admiral Burnett in the *Scylla* had arranged the escorts to provide a screen to protect the merchant ships, but it was inevitable some planes would get through. The German pilots, urged on by their victory against PQ17, had been asked to put in a 'special effort' to stop the Arctic convoys once and for all. They courageously kept formation against a wall of anti-aircraft fire. Inevitably, the ships' ordnance hit some aircraft, turning them into balls of flame or forcing them to plunge into the icy waters. But still they came on, trying to break the screen and get at the merchant ships beyond us.

I became aware of the ship lurching beneath me as she turned 45º to starboard, on orders from the *Scylla*. The ships were now facing our attackers, thereby reducing the target area, and making it easier to spot and avoid the tracks of approaching torpedoes.

Unfortunately, not all ships acted quickly enough or had heard the order to turn, as a wave of torpedoes sped towards them. The noise of explosions outside the turret sounded very close to where the *Milne* was positioned, we sailors inside feeling the surge of water under the ship. Still we continued to pound the skies with anti-aircraft fire, which joined the tracer and shells from the Oerlikons and Bofors.

And then, to the amazement of all of us on board, the ship seemed to slow to a stop. We had clearly not been hit, but something unusual was taking place.

Then the Petty Officer received new instructions through his headset. He ordered us outside, telling us we were needed amidships straight away.

Myself, Robbo and the rest of 'B' turret immediately stopped working and rushed to carry out the order, stepping outside on to the deck.

Now we were outside, the enormity of what was happening around us became apparent. A few hundred yards away a large cargo ship, the SS *Empire Stevenson*, having been engulfed in a huge explosion, was dead in the water and sinking rapidly. The force of the blast had severely damaged the ship sailing next to her, the SS *Wacosta*, which had then been hit by another torpedo and was also clearly sinking. In fact, ships were going down all around us, many of them having been hit by the torpedoes from the previous Luftwaffe run. I could see there were at least six ships in serious trouble.

Put to work immediately, teams from the *Milne* threw cargo nets over the side to pick up what survivors we could; and as the desperate men were hauled over the side, I was given the job of using cotton waste to clean oil from them. As the exhausted and injured men were laid out in a long line on the deck, the ship's doctor went down the line, checking to see who was still alive and which poor souls were beyond his help.

Two hundred yards away, a cargo ship was slowly sinking, stern first. I could see half a dozen of her crew climbing the forecastle in a bid to save themselves from going under with the ship. Some of them started to wave across to us, begging to be saved before the ice-cold waters of the Barents Sea enveloped them. There were only moments left before the whole ship would sink.

There was nothing any of us on board the *Milne* could do to save them, and we had to watch in horror as they were taken beneath the waves.

We were then given the order to take up our posts once more and rejoin the battle, effectively abandoning those in the water to their fate. The captain had taken a great risk in stopping the engines whilst such an action was going on, and his decision to restart them was purely in the interests of the safety of his own ship and crew. To stay still in the water for much longer, with a battle still raging all around us, would have made us an inviting target for the Luftwaffe or the U-boats.

Taking my position again, I had to put what I had witnessed to the back of my mind and get on with my job. I did it with more determination than ever. Being so close to the men who had perished and not being able to do a thing about it was upsetting and thoroughly depressing. But I had a job to do if we were going to stop more ships from going down.

Of the seven ships in the starboard column only one remained unscathed, and a further two in the middle of the convoy were also hit. As the smoke rose high into the afternoon sky, the German planes turned for home, leaving eight ships sinking to the bottom of the sea, taking down with them many sailors and the cargoes that were so desperately needed in Russia.

However, the convoy steamed on.

With the 'all clear' now sounding, I stepped out again from the turret and looked out to sea. There were now clear gaps in the columns where once merchantmen had sailed. There was an immense feeling of disappointment and sadness that we had been unable to stop the German torpedoes, but in my heart I knew we had done all we could to prevent the attack from succeeding.

It had been a sad day, but we knew it could have been much worse. There were still many ships powering on to Russia, and we had seen off a heavy and concerted attack from the best the Luftwaffe had to offer. Between us, we had managed to knock many planes out of the sky and we thought it unlikely they would come at us like that again.

However, this did not alleviate my feeling of sorrow at the loss of so many brave men. I looked to the merchant ships, and it was apparent to me just how poorly armed they were. It was up to us to keep them safe. We would just have to get as many through as we could.

We were then given the grim task of collecting the dog tags and pay books from the bodies of those men laid out on deck we had been unable to save.

As I carried out this sombre duty, I knew this was definitely the worst day of my whole life. Seeing the downhearted expression on my face, the Petty Officer reassured me there was nothing more any of us could have done and told us to try not to dwell on it.

Before we had any more time to ponder further the fate of the merchant sailors, 'action stations' sounded once again. Another few German planes had been spotted and were approaching the convoy from two sides. However, aware so many of their fellow pilots had fallen to the guns of the screen, they kept their distance and released their torpedoes from a distance, before turning and heading for home. I watched as the tracks of the torpedoes came closer, narrowly missing the destroyers and the *Scylla*, before their fuel ran out and they sank harmlessly to the bottom of the sea.

On returning to the turret, the Petty Officer had some information for us. We were told that, due to the rate of fire we had put up, we needed to limit the amount of shells we fired and the duration of any further barrages. The captain had ordered all the destroyers of the screen to do the same, for fear of running low on ammunition for the remainder of the journey. Our Petty Officer told us it appeared we had done our jobs too well, the rate being around twelve to fifteen rounds a minute, which was good going for the gunners.

Although thrilled at the compliment, the team knew this instruction made sense. The worst thing to happen would be to run out of shells and then come under air attack. We would all be sitting ducks. Captain Campbell knew his stuff, that was for certain.

This was not the only lesson learnt from the massed air assault that had just taken place. On board the *Avenger*, it was realized that launching the five Sea Hurricanes earlier had not been a good use of our limited air resources. It was decided in future they would not be sent into the sky until the enemy had committed to his mass assault, rather than sending them up piecemeal to chase away spotter planes or small numbers of enemy aircraft.

With the attacks over for now, the team was stood down. Now that I could relax for a while, I felt drained. My shipmates and I knew the Germans could return at any time and this was therefore a good opportunity to get some food and rest. Rushing to the mess deck, Robbo and I grabbed some corned beef sandwiches and a cup of kye. After eating what we could, we found a corner to lay our heads and the pair of us fell sound asleep.

It was not long before we were woken from our slumber as 'action stations' sounded once more throughout the ship. Within seconds we had negotiated the frozen decks and were again at our positions in 'B' turret, instantly alert and ready for action.

It was now 2030 hours and around a dozen He-111s had been spotted approaching the convoy. Following the direction of the gunnery officer, the team once more sprang into action and, as they had hours earlier, shells spouted from our twin 4.7 inch guns, adding to the barrage discharged in the direction of the oncoming aircraft.

It seemed they, too, like the second attack that afternoon, did not have the courage to come close, and they dropped their torpedoes too far away to have any impact on the convoy. However, a few planes did venture closer, some of which were knocked out of the sky by naval gunners.

As we observed the planes turning around and heading back to their bases, we pondered whether the Germans were starting to lose the will to fight. They were beginning to keep their distance and, with the escorts having shot down a good few of them earlier, might have become more apprehensive about getting too close. Maybe letting loose with such ferocity had made them think more carefully about their tactics.

There was no denying the logic. The massed attack earlier had seen the downing of numerous Nazi planes. It would take a brave pilot to fly so close to the destroyers again.

A few minutes later, the team and I were stood down and again we tried to clean up, eat and get some rest. The night was drawing in and the threat of further air attacks was diminishing. But we were by no means safe. The threat from the deep was constant, and the men working in the Electronic Warfare rooms on all the ships had their eyes fixed firmly to their Asdic screens, watching for the revealing 'pings' that would give away an enemy submarine.

At 0310 hours the following day I was woken by the noise of an explosion. At first disorientated, I made my way to the deck and looked out to the port side, where I was upset to see a tanker in one of the columns burning, lighting up the night sky with its flames. A huge pall of black smoke rose high into the starlit sky. A destroyer, I could not make out which one, was steaming out to meet her, no doubt to take off the crew before the ship sank.

I shivered. It was now getting extremely cold. Despite the thick thermal winter clothes we wore, the freezing Arctic weather was becoming as much a problem for the crew as the threat of the enemy. I looked across the ship and could see snow and ice forming in thick layers upon its decks, guns and gunwales. I knew what that meant. Between 'action stations', getting food and rest, and enemy attacks, I, along with the rest of the crew, would be called upon to break the ice from the ship. The threat of capsizing should the ship become top-heavy was very real. I had heard of ships on other convoys disappearing in the night, as if taken by an angry sea god, vanishing from the face of the earth. In reality, they had overturned, sinking to the bottom of the ocean, taking with them cargo and crew. I did not want to suffer the irony of fending off enemy planes and U-boats, only to lose my life because we had not taken care of the ship by clearing the decks. If and when they asked me to go outside and carry out this duty, I vowed I would do it without complaint.

Robbo stood beside me as we observed the destroyer take off the crew of the tanker. Someone told us it was the MV *Atheltemplar*, a British ship. This was something of a worry as she was one of the tankers that was to provide fuel for the other ships. We hoped we would have enough for the rest of the journey.

We watched in silence as, once the crew had been taken off the tanker, HMS *Tartar*, a Tribal-class destroyer, headed out to scuttle her with depth charges and gunfire.

We pondered just how the U-boat had got through the screen. It just went to show how alert we needed to be the whole time. We could not drop our guard at any point.

Throughout the night we were woken and called to 'action stations' as the 'wolf-pack' we knew to be out there harassed the convoy. But the U-boats were chased away almost as soon as they appeared on the Asdic screens, when the anti-submarine ships went out to find them.

* * *

The following morning, the escort scored its first success against the hidden foe. The U-boat *U589*, surfacing to charge her batteries, was spotted by a patrolling Swordfish from the *Avenger*. Dropping a smoke float to mark the U-boat's position, the Swordfish headed back to the safety of the convoy's guns after it was spotted and chased by a Ju-88. Believing the aerial threat was over, the captain of the submarine surfaced again to continue recharging his batteries, only to see HMS *Onslow* bearing down upon him. By the time he managed to dive again, it was too late. After *Onslow* had dropped a number of depth charges and chased what was nothing more than a dot and 'ping' on an Asdic screen, the *U589* finally disappeared from the *Onslow's* Asdic. That particular threat had been eliminated.

While the *Onslow* was hunting and destroying *U589*, the rest of the convoy came under another aerial attack. I was now losing count of the number of times we had been called to 'action stations'. The team and I were dead on our feet but still we were ready to fight on, the adrenalin coursing through our bodies in anticipation of providing another barrage.

This time the attack was roughly half the strength of the massed assault of the previous day. With the *Scylla* heading out in front to meet the planes head-on, turning in an arc to make it easier for all of her guns to be trained upon the approaching aircraft, the *Avenger*, tucked inside the screen, had readied six Hurricanes on the flight deck, their propellers turning, their pilots ready to go.

As the German planes, in two groups, reached the outer screen, the order was given to the destroyers to open up the barrage. Immediately, our team in 'B' turret got to work, pumping anti-aircraft shells into the air, mixing with the ordnance of the lighter weaponry of all the ships. As one of the Luftwaffe groups concentrated on the *Scylla* and ships providing the screen, the other turned its attention to the carrier, HMS *Avenger*. Due to the noise, and our concentration on carrying out our tasks, we were unaware the Hurricanes had taken to the skies and were now attacking the He-111s and Ju-88s, forcing them away or knocking them out of the sky.

Inside the turret, the noise was horrendous. The rate of fire was fast, and the constant boom as the 4.7 inch shells exited the barrels, combined with all the other noise of battle, tested the endurance of us all. But we were not to be found wanting. Methodically we worked, listening to the shouted instructions of the PO, our concentration total as I aligned the pointer to the required marking, the orders coming thick and fast as the range and position changed every few seconds.

It was not long before it was over. We breathed a collective sigh of relief as the brief skirmish came to an end. Word got around this had been another triumph for the convoy and the escort screen that our ship, HMS *Milne*, the flotilla leader, had been a part of. The attack had been a complete failure on the part of the Germans. Not a single ship had been hit, and eleven enemy planes now lay at the bottom of the Barents Sea, knocked out of the sky by the heavy fusillade we had provided and the skills of the Hurricane pilots.

Thinking the enemy had by now learned their lesson, the exhilarated crew of the *Milne* enjoyed a brief respite. After the empty shell cases had been removed from the turret, soup and sandwiches were delivered to us at our posts.

With a 'well done' message from Captain Campbell still ringing in our ears, the 'action stations' sounded yet again.

'For God's sake,' said Robbo, throwing his soup over the deck and hastily stuffing the remains of a corned beef sandwich into his mouth. 'Will these fellas ever learn.'

I grinned. The nerves of the very first attack the previous day had now left me and I went about my business in a professional and methodical way. It had been proved that if each man carried out the instructions of our officers and operated the machinery according to how we had been trained, everything would turn out well. Even though most of the crew had been new to the Royal Navy, none of us could be considered green 'newbies' any more. We were fully fledged combat veterans. Boys had turned into men.

Above the clouds, out of sight of the crews below, a group of bombers had appeared on the radar screens.

For over an hour, with each break in the clouds, a bomber would descend upon the convoy, drop its payload and then climb once more into the cover of the clouds. This form of attack proved as fruitless as the last, with no ships being hit. However, our barrage was only able to bring down one more aircraft.

No sooner had the bombers left than another massed attack of planes approached from the south. This was becoming relentless, and the activity on board all the destroyers was frantic as we gunners adjusted our sights and once more pounded the skies. Mixed in with our barrage were more Sea Hurricanes who went out to meet the Germans.

Again, it looked like the target for the Luftwaffe was the carrier HMS *Avenger*, as the He-111s swarmed towards her, pursued by the Hurricanes who flew through the escort's barrage, heroically ignoring the shell bursts around them as they attempted to stop the German planes from hitting the carrier. By some miracle, none of the torpedoes struck their intended targets, and many planes crashed into the sea, cut down by our fusillade or shot down by the Hurricanes.

By the time the attack was over, and the surviving Luftwaffe planes had headed for home, three Hurricanes had crashed into the sea and nine more German planes had been consigned to a watery grave.

However, nobody was about to cheer another success. One of the torpedoes had got through the screen and hit the SS *Mary Luckenbach*, a US cargo ship in the somewhat jinxed starboard column. The merchantman was carrying a cargo of 1,000 tons of TNT, which exploded in a huge fireball, ripping the ship apart, wiping out the entire crew of forty-one and killing a further twenty-four United States Navy Armed Guard marines. As the pall of smoke rose high into the crisp September sky, the ship bobbed on the surface for a few moments before sinking to the depths below.

Despite the loss of the *Mary Luckenbach*, the earlier sinking of the *U589* and the successful repelling of the air attacks provided a huge surge in the morale of the convoy. It proved the combined actions of the air and surface escort could yield excellent results. There was no doubt that this convoy, although coming under sustained enemy attack, was proving PQ17 had been something of a one-off. As long as escorts were organized, consisted of the right numbers and had air support, there was no reason why the convoys could not get through with the majority of their cargo unmolested.

For the remainder of the day the convoy was harried by the occasional Ju-88 dropping its bombs through holes in the cloud, but none of them landed on their targets, and the escort was easily able to fend them off. However, there was no chance for the crews to relax, the threat ever constant from the air and from beneath the waves.

There was also another significant danger: surface ships.

On 14 September, the Admiralty got word the *Tirpitz* had left harbour at Trondheim and was now unable to be located. Should she be heading to Altenfjord, (only 270 nautical miles from Bear Island, to the south-west of the convoy's present position), to rendezvous with the battleships *Scheer*, *Hipper* and *Köln*, then they could wreak havoc with the convoy. This kept every sailor on every ship at a heightened sense of alert. As it happened, the intelligence was incorrect and the ship had never left her base. This false report was reminiscent of the previous convoy, when the ships were ordered to scatter, fearing an attack from the *Tirpitz*. This time, common sense prevailed and no such order was sent

The convoy steamed on.

CHAPTER SEVEN

Fire and Ice

PQ18 had now passed Bear Island and was on the final run towards the Kola Inlet. So far, we had lost nine merchant ships.

It was evening and the light was getting low. I took the chance to settle down and attempt to get some sleep. Looking at my crewmates I could see they were probably feeling the same way as I was: cold, hungry and thoroughly exhausted. We had been on heightened alert for the last few days and had spent the majority of them at some form of 'action stations'. There had been no chance to relax, to shower or to eat anything hot, having had to make do with a seemingly endless supply of corned beef sandwiches and cups of kye whenever we got the chance. After each duty, we would simply grab a bite to eat and crash out anywhere we could find a space.

However, these periods of rest were often broken by the sound of 'action stations' as an Asdic operator somewhere in the fleet alerted his superiors to a 'ping' that had appeared on his screen, indicating a U-boat might be close by.

Between air attacks there was still work to be done. The guns, after a sustained period of use such as they had never had before, needed to be cleaned, serviced and made ready for the next attack, its arrival just a matter of when, not if. The lack of proper sleep gave rise to the worry that, as we became more exhausted, our performance might slacken. It was imperative that this should not happen. We needed to be as efficient now as we had been when the convoy first set sail.

The night of 14 September passed without major incident, and the sun rose to a cold and wet day. Snow and sleet blew into those on deck, and the temperature in 'B' turret was more akin to a fridge than a warship. Wrapped up in our thick duffel coats, heavy sweaters and thermal mittens, bulked out with all this clothing and identifiable only through the eyelets of our balaclavas, we found it awkward to move and operate the equipment.

But after hours of experiencing these conditions, we were still confident we could do a good job.

By now the convoy was over 400 miles from the nearest Luftwaffe base at Banak, so no attack was expected until around midday; if the German planes took off at the break of dawn, it would take them that long to reach the convoy. As if on cue, at around 1245 hours, the familiar sight of enemy aircraft appeared in the skies to the south.

Immediately, Sea Hurricanes went up to harass them. They were going to make sure this was another wasted trip for the Germans.

In groups of only three, the He-111s and Ju-88s occasionally broke through holes in the cloud to attempt an attack, but immediately the guns from the destroyers opened up, forcing them to drop their bombs woefully short or return once again to the cover of the clouds, where the Hurricanes were waiting for them.

This went on for nearly three hours before the Germans, low on fuel, finally gave up and the last flight headed for home, jettisoning their bombs in the process. However, they were now three fewer in number than when they had set out.

To me and my comrades on board the *Milne* this had been easy compared to the attacks of the previous few days, and we wondered whether the Germans were now losing the will to go on. The pilots of the downed planes would never see home again and, with the combined firepower of the destroyers, and the spirit, endurance and courage of the Hurricane pilots, it was no wonder they had kept their distance.

There was a short scare later in the day, when the crew of HMS *Opportune*, operating at the edge of the convoy, thought they had spotted surface ships on the horizon. They set out to investigate and found that, instead of the dreaded *Tirpitz*, it was a couple of U-boats. As they were so far away from the convoy and posing no immediate threat, it was decided to leave them alone for now.

The cold was becoming a serious problem. We could not stay out on an open deck for long, and I was happy with the shelter the turret provided. However, during early evening, sitting in the mess deck with Robbo and a few others, we were approached by our Chief Petty Officer.

He told us we were needed for an important task and were to wrap up warm. He said we had no choice in the matter and there was to be no arguing about it. We knew what this meant.

Putting on my duffel coat, mittens and woolly hat, along with the others I took one of the tools he handed to us. They were a mixture of picks, mauls and hammers from a supply that had been deposited in the mess deck and, once we were all suitably attired, we followed him outside.

Once on deck, we connected ourselves to a hawser line. The last thing anyone wanted to do was to fall overboard. That would be fatal.

The snow and sleet that had been falling on the convoy all day had now frozen to form large patches of ice on the deck, guns and superstructure. As we all knew, it was extremely important this was broken off and thrown overboard. If it was allowed to build up too much, it could even cause the ship to capsize. This could not be allowed to happen.

For the next thirty minutes, myself, Robbo and the rest of the team smashed at the ice on the guns and decks and swept the snow and broken ice over the side into the water. We looked across to the other ships and could see working parties like ours doing the same. If there was one thing that was true, we were all in this together. It was tiring work for already bone-weary men, but we went at it nevertheless, even with a cheery attitude at times, despite the snow and sleet still falling and blowing into our faces.

At one point, one of the lads began to sing 'Oh, I do like to be beside the seaside', and we joined in with his ironic choice of song. I even asked the Chief if he could get permission from the Captain for us to put a couple of deck chairs out so we could enjoy the weather. He replied that he would certainly do that but that we all had to ensure we wore our caps to avoid sunburn.

This cheery attitude managed to make the job a little more bearable, and after our duty was done we trudged back to the sanctuary of the mess deck, where we handed our tools on to the next group who had been gathered to relieve us.

The rest of the evening passed without incident, and Robbo and I were finally able to get some rest.

At 0300 hours the following morning, while I was sleeping, the Asdic operators aboard HMS *Impulsive* picked up a U-boat contact, just outside her screening position ahead of the convoy. She set off to investigate. Whether this was one of the two spotted by the *Opportune* some hours before was unknown, but *Impulsive* had time to drop a number of depth charges before the convoy caught up. After it had passed over, the *Impulsive* then looked to continue her search for the elusive submarine. However, she did not need to bother, as a large amount of debris and oil was spotted on the surface, confirming the kill. (This was later identified as the *U457*, which sank with all hands.)

At 0900 hours the ships turned to starboard and headed south, towards the Kola Inlet. A Catalina aircraft from a squadron based in northern Russia was spotted. The appearance of this aircraft meant the duties of the Swordfish pilots, insofar as PQ18 was concerned, had now come to an end; the Catalinas would provide U-boat search cover for the convoy on the final miles to Murmansk.

Later that afternoon, the destroyer escort, including HMS *Milne*, together with the aircraft carrier HMS *Avenger* and the flagship HMS *Scylla*, were ordered to detach ourselves from the convoy and rendezvous with the returning ships of QP14.

As we turned away from those ships we had sailed alongside for the past few days, I watched from the gunwale and raised my hand in farewell. Whether anyone saw me or not, I was not sure, but I wished them 'bon voyage' and hoped they would get to their destination safely. I felt a closeness to the men on those ships and knew PQ18's would be a journey I would remember for the rest of my life.

PQ18 would continue on for a few more days, escorted by the remaining Allied ships and two Russian destroyers, *Gremyashchi* and *Sokrushiteini*, which sailed out to meet them the following day. Fighters from the Russian Air Force would provide aerial cover for the remainder of the journey now the *Avenger* had gone.

However, a further two Allied merchant ships were sunk after coming under aerial attack on the final run to Archangel. Out of the forty merchant ships that had set sail, twenty-eight arrived to deliver their vital cargoes.

PQ18 was hailed as a success. After the debacle of PQ17 and the loss of the majority of the merchantmen on that convoy, the fact that so many ships had got through this time showed that successful Arctic convoys were still very achievable, as long as they had a strong escort.

The destroyer escort that had been detached on 16 September now had new orders. We were to protect the men and ships of the returning convoy QP14, many of whom had had a very eventful journey on the way in.

We were headed for home.

CHAPTER EIGHT

Homeward Bound

We were headed for home all right, but it was not going to be an easy ride.

The Luftwaffe and the U-boat 'wolf packs' were still out there and continued to be a major threat, despite the returning merchant vessels being empty of cargo, having delivered their loads at Murmansk and Archangel. On board many of the returning ships were the survivors of the ill-fated PQ17, which had been left unprotected after the order was given to scatter on the evening of 4 July. For two months these sailors, having gone through what must have been a frozen hell on earth, were made to endure the monotony of waiting in Archangel to be escorted back to Britain. The amenities at the Russian port were virtually non-existent, and with nothing to do other than sit around in the cold, these men were desperate to get home.

Having set out from Archangel on 13 September, QP14 had thus far been left alone by the Germans. During this time the enemy had been concentrating their efforts on the ships of PQ18 rather than directing their attention to empty vessels. There would be time for that later. After all, they still had a very long way to go and would be within their sights long after PQ18 had either been obliterated or had reached the sanctuary of port.

Although it was a good feeling to be heading for the safety of British waters, my shipmates and I were aware we had to remain on high alert during the trip back. Even though we were essentially escorting empty ships, the Germans would still want to sink them, to stop them returning with more supplies at a later date. They would also want to exact revenge for the majority of PQ18 getting through, and for having suffered such a great loss of aircraft and U-boats in their efforts to stop us.

Once the convoy was formed up, we set sail westwards, heading on a course that would take us just south of Spitzbergen. En route, the convoy encountered intermittent fog, along with driving snow that chilled the crews to the bone. The only positive we could take from this was that air attack in these conditions was highly unlikely. However, some enemy aircraft had been spotted and, the following day, escorting Swordfish reported U-boats had been sighted prowling the area in search of prey.

At my position in the gun turret I shivered. It was bitterly cold this far north. We were sailing very close to the ice barrier, and the crew had to constantly go outside during our stand-down periods to shift snow and ice from the decks. Along with my friends, I longed for the day when we would be sailing in milder waters.

When I had wanted to join the Navy I had envisaged warmer climes, feeling the sun on my face as I visited wonderfully exotic ports and enjoyed all the delights they had to offer. One day, I thought, maybe one day.

I shook myself from this reverie and looked out to sea. The weather had turned milder and the sun was starting to shine through the clouds. To starboard I could make out huge icebergs, an icy mist clinging to their bases, where the sea lapped gently against them. They gave me the impression they were almost alive, skulking in the calm water, waiting for an unfortunate ship to crash against them, just like the SS *Titanic* had done thirty years earlier. It was a magnificent thing to behold, and when the sun reflected off them they could be quite dazzling, forcing us sailors to shield our eyes when we looked upon them.

As the convoy steamed on we passed the ironically named Hope Island, an uninhabited lump of rock in the middle of the Arctic Ocean. I was reminded just how desolate this part of the world was. Cold, empty, lonely and thoroughly depressing.

I was aware of Swordfish aircraft in the air to the front of the convoy, on the lookout for U-boats. Along with a number of other destroyers, the *Milne* took up position astern to provide a screen against any enemy submarines that might be following behind. We had no idea which route the Admiral had set, but it soon became clear we were heading as far away from the Luftwaffe bases as we could, before presumably turning and heading south for the safe haven of Iceland.

The threat from the air seemed to be diminishing with every mile covered, and I was finally able to relax a little. The return journey was proving to be a lot less fraught than what we had become used to. However, despite the convoy's best efforts to keep the U-boats at bay, just before dawn on 20 September there was an almighty explosion as torpedoes struck the minesweeper HMS *Leda*, which was part of the screen, not far from the *Milne*'s position. The crew managed to abandon ship, and she sank shortly afterward. Despite the best efforts of the escort, the submarine responsible, the *U435*, managed to get away.

With Swordfish patrolling the sky almost constantly, the U-boats stayed underwater for fear of being spotted. With such a large escort presence providing a formidable screen, it came as a huge surprise when another of the 'wolf pack' managed to break through undetected and slam two torpedoes into the side of the US merchant ship *Silver Sword*.

As smoke rose high into the air, observing from the shelter of the turret, I could not understand what had happened. I could make out lifeboats being lowered into the ocean and was happy to see the crew getting off the stricken vessel safely.

I asked how this had happened when there were so many ships providing cover. I was informed by someone who seemed to know that on occasion the Asdic did not work properly. This was due to the sea conditions, something to do with the temperature of the water and the way sound waves bounce off it. When these conditions occurred, U-boats could pass close by without being detected. I did not fully understand the explanation, but it showed us that the Asdic was not foolproof and we had to remain vigilant at all times.

I sighed. I felt for those boys on the merchant ship. She had been one of those that had survived PQ17, her crew waiting for weeks on end in Archangel for the trip home, and now, as she floundered, awaiting the *coup de grâce* to be given by the Royal Navy destroyer, HMS *Worcester*, I felt an immense sadness for the ship and those who had sailed in her.

Despite the efforts of the anti-submarine ships, the offending U-boat slipped the net and could not be found.

An hour later, as dusk was drawing closer, there was an announcement over the tannoy system. It was Captain Campbell.

He told us that we were to have a very special visitor to the ship. The Admiral was swapping the *Scylla* for the *Milne*. We were to run alongside the *Scylla* shortly, when he would be transferred across to us. The Captain explained that this was an honour for the ship and he wanted us to show the Admiral what an excellent and professional crew we were. All free hands were then ordered to form up on the starboard side to receive him.

I turned to the Petty Officer and asked him what he thought it was all about. He replied that he had no idea but he was sure there was a good reason for it. We all deduced that the *Scylla* was probably leaving the convoy but Burnett wanted to stay on.

Having been stood down from the turret gun, I made my way to the side of the ship as ordered and watched patiently as the *Scylla* and the *Milne* came together. The ships were travelling at a rate of around 14 knots. We could not stop to do the transfer as this would have made it easy for any trailing U-boat to get a clear shot at the ships, an opportunity no submarine commander worth his salt would pass up. Skilfully the two ships were brought together, and I could see a mass of sailors on the port side of the *Scylla*, all cheering and waving at their colleagues on the *Milne*. It was good to see so many different faces, and the occasion produced an immediate improvement in morale, this being a welcome break from the tribulations of war.

A rope was thrown across from the *Milne* to the *Scylla*, where a couple of sailors attached a hawser line. Once fastened, all available hands hauled the hawser across and it was quickly attached to the ship's crane. Next, a metal bosun's chair was secured to the hawser on the *Scylla's* side, and Burnett now stepped out of the bridge, after bidding goodbye to the duty officers.

The Rear Admiral was easy to spot. Wearing full uniform and a cap that managed to stay on his head despite the wind, he was assisted into the bosun's chair, and at the order 'Haul away' was lifted into the air and out and over the gap between the two ships. Everyone on both sides cheered, and when I looked across to the *Scylla's* bridge I could see the officers smiling and one or two openly laughing. The situation was comical. At one point the ships hit a swell and the Admiral was lost from sight for a moment as the chair dipped lower than desired, hovering only a few feet over the surface of the sea. Everyone held their breath. It would be too much if he was somehow drowned by his own side. However, he was quickly back in view as the waves rose again and the crane swung him over the deck and on to the *Milne*, where a group of sailors released him from the chair to the sound of the boatswain's pipes. After all, an admiral was coming on board, and certain naval etiquette still needed to be upheld, no matter the circumstances.

A few moments later, the Rear Admiral's flag was raised at the masthead and the *Scylla* broke away from the *Milne*, setting a course away from the convoy. I was surprised to see that *Avenger* was also leaving us. When I returned to the mess deck I mentioned it to Robbo, who surmised that we were probably close enough to home for the RAF to look after us now.

He was partly right. The decision to release *Scylla* and *Avenger* from the convoy was to avoid presenting them as a target to any U-boat commander wanting to make a name for himself. The convoy was moving slowly, and the aerial threat had now diminished to the point that only an occasional spotter plane had been sighted as we pulled further and further from the range of the enemy's Norwegian bases. As the weather was also becoming thicker, the chance of further air attack was pretty much over. However, with U-boats still known to be operating in the area, the removal of the *Avenger* with her submarine-hunting Swordfish aircraft caused one or two frowns on the faces of the sailors. Having flown endless back-to-back sorties, their pilots were now totally exhausted, and Rear Admiral Burnett had taken the decision to release them from their duties now that RAF Coastal Command could take up their role.

However, Coastal Command was stretched. Providing cover for the Atlantic convoys as they entered the Northern and Western Approaches, they were thin on the ground when it came to taking on the added responsibility of looking after the returning empty ships of QP14. Although they could provide some cover, it was not at the same level as that given by the Swordfish of the *Avenger*.

The following day, 21 September, a Catalina arrived and immediately set to work hunting for U-boats. It was a welcome sight, but after sustaining damage early on, it was forced to land in the sea, leaving the convoy with no air support whatsoever. With only the Asdic now available to detect any 'wolf packs', it was not long before calamity struck.

Providing part of the screen on the port side of the convoy, HMS *Somali*, a Tribal-class destroyer, was torpedoed by a U-boat that had got ahead of us. Despite a huge hole in her side, she did not sink, and Rear Admiral Burnett, watching events from the bridge of the *Milne*, sent out the destroyer HMS *Ashanti* to take her under tow. Burnett also ordered a number of the escort ships to provide protection for the two destroyers, leaving the convoy's own escort somewhat depleted. However, as we were protecting only fifteen returning merchantmen, he felt what was left was sufficient to see them home safely.

Burnett, wanting to see for himself the damage to the *Somali* close up, ordered the *Milne* to approach the ship. Watching from the gunwale, I looked on as the ships came closer. There was a large hole in the hull, the torpedo having hit her amidships, wrecking the engine room. I could see men inside working hard to repair the damage. From what I could make out, the ship would now be unable to make it to port without the assistance of the vessels Burnett had assigned to her. Having made his decisions and issued the orders, the Rear Admiral ordered the *Milne* to return to the convoy, and we carried on.

As we headed back to the convoy the 'action stations' sounded and we war-weary sailors again jumped to our positions. I had by now lost count of the number of times this had happened. It was becoming routine, normal almost. I looked to the sky but could see no planes.

Although the threat from the air was almost certainly gone, there was still a sense of nervousness abounding in regard to the submarine menace. With the *Somali* having been hit, there was a realization amongst the crew of the *Milne* that anything was possible.

We presumed that a sub had been spotted and we made ready. Maybe we could get a shot at her before she dived.

The *Milne* steamed on at full speed. Word reached us that a U-boat had indeed been spotted, approximately four miles away, and we mentally prepared ourselves for a fight. A group of sailors manned the depth charges, priming them ready to be released. I and the rest of the team prepared ourselves in the gun turret, ready to fire on it should it resurface and want to put up a fight. This was very different to how I had felt during the air attacks, when the enemy could clearly be seen in the sky. This time they were below us, to all intents and purposes invisible. It was now up to the boys at the Asdic screens to locate the U-boat.

Whether or not it was again the result of sea conditions, which were very calm, and the explanation Robbo had given me earlier about how the varying temperature of the water could play havoc with the Asdic equipment, after an hour of hunting the area, the order was given to stand down. We had lost it. The U-boat had got away.

For the next day and night the convoy continued on unmolested. On the morning of 22 September, Rear Admiral Burnett gave the order for the *Milne* to leave the convoy and proceed to Seidisfjord in Iceland, to rendezvous with the *Scylla*; he could then be transferred back to his own ship. Being so close to home, it was assumed that no further attacks would take place and the convoy would have enough cover without the protection of the *Milne*.

As the ship broke away and steamed at full speed ahead, leaving QP14 in its wake, I felt a real sense of achievement. This had been my first voyage and it had been extremely eventful. Although some merchantmen had been lost, it would still be considered a success. There were enough positives to take from the journey that the Arctic convoys would be able to continue and our allies in Russia could fight on. With the might of Russia and with America on Britain's side since Pearl Harbor, it would be a case of when the war was won, not if.

However, I knew there was a long way to go yet before any kind of victory could be declared. As Iceland came into view, I sighed to myself. For the first time in what felt like a very long time, at last I felt safe again.

* * *

Shortly after the *Milne* left the convoy, QP14 again came under attack from U-boats. In quick succession, the merchant ships *Ocean Voice* and *Bellingham* and the tanker *Grey Ranger* were torpedoed and sunk. All the crew of both cargo ships were rescued successfully, but the *Grey Ranger* lost six men. The convoy arrived in Iceland on 26 September.

Limping behind on a tow line, having been torpedoed near Jan Mayen Island, HMS *Somali*, together with the ships escorting her, hit heavy weather on 25 September. Although desperate efforts were made to save the ship and her crew, she sank, taking down with her thirty-five brave sailors. A further sixty-seven were rescued from the icy waters.

This incident showed what a lottery sailing on the convoys could be. At any time, a U-boat could break through the protective screen undetected and unleash death upon any of the ships it chose. It was down to luck, and the grace of God, which ships that would be.

CHAPTER NINE

Operation Torch

Although PQ18 had not reached Murmansk completely intact, it was considered a major success, and the Russian convoys were to continue. Thousands of tons of war materiel had been delivered to the Soviets, boosting their efforts in the struggle against the Nazi invaders. HMS *Milne*, having arrived in Scapa Flow after leaving the convoy on 22 September, was to receive news that would boost our already high morale. King George VI was to visit the Home Fleet to pass on his congratulations, and the *Milne*, being the flotilla leader, was to head to Thurso to receive him on board and bring him to the fleet at anchor in Scapa. This was a huge honour for the crew and gave us the sense that what we had gone through on PQ18 was being appreciated, not only by the public but also by those in high positions.

HMS *Milne* was not the only ship the King was to visit in what was to be a busy day for him. He was to be received aboard other vessels that had taken part in the journey to Russia, to acknowledge the sacrifice made by the men of the Royal and Merchant Navies.

On the day itself, the ship's company, having cleaned the ship to as high a standard as we could so soon after an action, formed up on the decks to receive the monarch. Standing in line with my shipmates, I watched as the launch in which King George was travelling headed in our direction, cutting through the choppy waters effortlessly. For a few moments it was lost from our view as the King was assisted on to the steps that had been lowered, allowing him to board the ship from the starboard side.

Then I heard the familiar sound of the boatswain's pipes as the King, dressed in naval uniform, stepped on board, to be greeted by Captain Campbell and other senior officers. They immediately made their way to the open bridge, from where the dignitaries and officers could view the ship and its company.

I realized I was smiling. This would be a wonderful tale to tell Annette the next time I saw her.

From where I was on deck, I could see the King chatting and looking on as Captain Campbell answered his questions and pointed out the features of the *Milne*. I strained my neck to see as much of the man as I could. This was a day I would remember for the rest of my life. After all, it wasn't every day the monarch visited your home. For that was what HMS *Milne* was to me now: my home. And as I looked along the line of sailors standing with me, I realized these men were my family. The war had brought us together to form a bond that could never be broken.

Not long after the King had boarded, we were underway, sailing the short distance back to Scapa Flow and to the other ships awaiting his visit. On arrival, I could see many ships lying at anchor, their crews on deck and wearing their best uniforms.

As the King left the *Milne* some time later, three cheers were called, and he turned to acknowledge the salute. He then gave the order to 'splice the mainbrace', the instruction for an extra tot of rum to be delivered to all the crew. A few moments later, he boarded a launch with his entourage and was off on the next leg of his inspection.

No sooner had the King departed the ship than the *Milne* set course once more for Thurso. This time we were to pick up another VIP and bring him to Scapa Flow. It was the Prime Minister, Winston Churchill.

Again, once Churchill was on board, the crew formed up for inspection. As he was led on a tour of the ship, the sailors craned their necks to catch sight of the man who was leading the country through its darkest times. Having only previously seen him on newsreels and heard his voice over the radio, each of us wanted to get a good look at him.

The *Milne* set course back to Scapa with their second VIP of the day on board, and after he left the ship, it was clear the morale of the crew had been boosted. With these two visits, we knew whatever we had endured on PQ18, and whatever might come in the future, we had the full support and appreciation of both the British people and the government.

All in all, it had been a most successful day, the Captain passing on his thanks to the crew in a short address later that evening.

Gibraltar, November 1942

Although it was technically winter, you could have been forgiven for thinking it was the height of summer. The sun shone brightly on the deck of HMS *Milne* and reflected back off the gentle waves as they lapped against the ship's hull. Matelots, now without the duffel coats and woolly hats we had become accustomed to recently, went about their duties in shirtsleeves, and some of us even wandered around shirtless, enjoying the Mediterranean heat on our skin. Officers allowed us to relax and enjoy the respite. After all, we deserved it. We had proved ourselves worthy of a little downtime and, whilst we were in dock, the strictness of normal discipline was relaxed a little.

HMS *Milne* had been ordered to leave the Home Fleet and make her way to Gibraltar to form part of the escort for Operation Torch, the invasion of North Africa, arriving on 5 November. Along with other destroyers we were to form part of 'Force H', to protect the troopships and landing craft from attack by the Italian, German and Vichy French navies.

To me and my pals this was a far cry from a few short weeks ago when the ship had braved the hazards of the Arctic Ocean. This was a period to be enjoyed.

Arriving on a very warm day, the ship pulled up against the jetty and was secured with ropes. A gangplank was then rigged so that anyone with permission to leave the ship could easily walk ashore. Those on duty assembled on the forecastle to enjoy the sunshine, myself included. One of the officers had a camera and asked us to arrange ourselves in a large group for a photograph. After all, a record needed to be made for posterity.

Once the photograph had been taken, I looked out across the bay to the assembled ships. Whatever was coming was going to be big, I thought. Cruisers and destroyers, mixed with troopships and a myriad of other smaller vessels, filled the bay, the sun bouncing off their grey hulls and superstructures. It was a sight to behold. I thought PQ18 had been big, but the fleet gathered here almost dwarfed it.

With a few days to go before the operation was to take place, and with the ship ready for action, the officers were aware that the crew, despite enjoying the sunshine, might get a little restless. It was decided by Captain Campbell to allow the men some proper rest and relaxation, and so permission was given for a run ashore.

Robbo and I were lucky enough to be in the first group allowed to go and see the sights of Gibraltar. As we set out just after midday, I smiled to myself. This was one of the things I had been most looking forward to since joining the Navy.

I looked up at the huge rock that dominated the skyline. It seemed more magnificent the closer we got to it, but it was not the seeing of sights that most appealed to me. It was a month before my nineteenth birthday, and I was intent on celebrating it right now. After all, who knew where I would be on the actual day. And so, a group of us from the *Milne* set off in search of a good pub in which to spend our afternoon.

A few minutes later, our group of sailors were walking purposefully along Main Street. Seeing a building with the sign 'Universal Bar' on the corner of Horse Bank Parade, we entered. It was a large pub compared to others we had passed, with a long bar, above which a four-piece band was playing quite loud music from a balcony, forcing us to raise our voices when we spoke. I was surprised to see the band comprised four young women. A banner behind them declared 'Free Drinks to Everyone on Victory Night'.

The bar was already starting to get busy despite it being only early afternoon, as sailors from many of the ships docked in the harbour enjoyed the freedom their captains had granted them. It was noisy, full of cigarette smoke and everyone seemed in good cheer. I knew immediately this was the place for me. Pushing past a couple of burly sailors, I made my way to the bar, Robbo and the others following closely behind. I could see a large number of staff working behind the bar, struggling to keep up with the orders, whilst others moved quickly between tables collecting glasses. I wondered if they had been given prior notice the ships were coming in and knew they would be in for a very busy few days.

I got to the bar and ordered some beers from a pretty young barmaid. As she was pouring them I nodded towards the balcony, where the four women were playing a loud jazz number, and asked her what was going on. She replied they were very popular and joked that they were up there out of the way of us rowdy lot. As I took the beers, she told us we were in luck today and spirits were only fourpence a shot, which came as very welcome news.

Charlie as a young child, with his father, Harry and sister, Annette, c.1928.
(*Charlie Erswell*)

Memorial postcard commemorating the visit of Edward, Prince of Wales, to
Berwick-upon-Tweed, to open the Royal Tweed Bridge on 16 May 1928. (*Anne
Moore, Keeper of Collections, Museums Northumberland*)

Charlie, (front, second from right) with friends, Harrogate, c.1940. (*Charlie Erswell*)

Charlie (front, right) with GPO colleagues, Cairn Hydro Hotel, Harrogate, c.1941. (*Charlie Erswell*)

Above left: Max Karo in First World War uniform. Charlie joined the cadet force led by him in 1940.

Above right: Annette Erswell, Charlie's sister. (*Charlie Erswell*)

Below: HMS *Ganges* front entrance. (*Raphael Tuck & Sons postcard*)

HMS *Ganges* drill yard, where Charlie did his basic training. (*Raphael Tuck & Sons postcard*)

Christmas Day, 1941, HMS *Ganges* recruit course. Charlie, aged eighteen, is front row, far left. (*Charlie Erswell*)

Right: Charlie in Royal Navy uniform.
(*Charlie Erswell*)

Below: HMS *Milne*, M-Class destroyer.
Charlie was the turret trainer in
B turret, just in front of the bridge.
(*flickriver.com*)

HMS *Milne* gun crew in front of A turret, c.1942. Charlie is far left, front row. (*Charlie Erswell*)

About to clear the deck of ice, HMS *Milne*, PQ18. Charlie is third from right, hatless. (*Charlie Erswell*)

Charlie and shipmates clearing the deck of ice and snow, PQ18. If this was not done, there was a danger of the ship becoming top heavy and capsizing. (*Charlie Erswell*)

Heinkel He-111 bombers of the Luftwaffe. A massed attack of these aircraft sank many merchant ships on 13 September 1942, during convoy PQ18. (*Bundesarchiv, Bild 101I-408-0847-10 / Martin / CC-BY-SA 3.0*)

Left: PQ18. HMS *Milne,* frozen deck. (*Charlie Erswell*)

Below: PQ18 under attack. (*pinterest*)

Above: The SS *Mary Luckenbach*, carrying 1,000 tonnes of TNT, burns after being hit by Luftwaffe bombs, 13 September, 1942. Picture taken from flight deck of HMS *Avenger*. (*seafarers.org*)

Right: Charlie, near to Polyarny, 1942. Note how the background has been obliterated by the censor (who was the ship's doctor). (*Charlie Erswell*)

Sailors clearing ice from the foredeck of HMS *Milne*, September 1942. (*Charlie Erswell*)

HMS *Milne* crew, prior to Operation Torch, Gibraltar, November 1942. Charlie is centre, partly obscured. (*Charlie Erswell*)

US troops wading ashore during Operation Torch, North Africa, November 1942. (*pinterest*)

Fairey Swordfish anti-submarine aircraft. These aircraft were used with some success against U-boats during the convoys. (*history.net*)

The destroyer HMS *Savage*. Charlie's second ship, on which he worked in the director above the bridge.

View from HMS *Sheffield*'s bridge, convoy JW53. The roof of one of the gun turrets was ripped off in the high winds, causing her to return to Iceland for repairs. (*Bundesarchiv*)

Convoy JW53 sailing through ice floes in the Barents Sea, February 1943. (*IWM*)

Royal Navy ships en route to Normandy, D-Day, 6 June 1944. (*dday-overlord.com*)

Crown Prince Olaf greets crowds on his return to Oslo, 15 May 1945. His bodyguard, the famous saboteur Max Manus, can be seen in the front seat holding a Thompson sub-machine gun. (*reddit*)

The SS *Winchester Victory*, Charlie's first ship in the Merchant Navy. (*Fred Barr Collection, Stewart Bell Jr, Archives Room, Handley Regional Library, Winchester, VA, USA*)

Charlie's shore leave pass whilst at Port Said with the SS *Winchester Victory*. (*Charlie Erswell*)

Above left: Charlie and pal aboard the SS *Winchester Victory*, Port Said, Egypt, 1946. (*Charlie Erswell*)

Above right: Mick, Charlie's best friend when serving on the SS *Winchester Victory*. Together they swam the harbour at Valletta, Malta, after a night of drinking. (*Charlie Erswell*)

Receiving the Ushakov medal from Russian dignitaries aboard HMS *Belfast*, London, 9 May 2014. (*Keith Nisbet Photography, Woking*)

Charlie Erswell, VE Day, 8 May 2020, aged ninety-six. (*Charlie Erswell*)

The drinks were served in tin cans that had their sharp edges bent over. There were two reasons for this. The first was to prevent the consumer from cutting his lip whilst drinking, and the second was so that, should trouble break out, they could not be used as weapons.

We looked around the room and saw a table free in the corner, next to a bunch of Americans and Canadians. Sitting down, our group grinned to each other and raised our cans. Robbo toasted the *Milne*, raised his drink to his lips and gulped down the full contents in one go. Slamming the can down on the table, he stood up and declared he was going to get another round in.

A few hours later, as the band played 'God Save The Queen', in a probable attempt to let us all know our time was now up and we had to leave, a fight broke out among some sailors across the room. This quickly spread to other tables and, not knowing exactly how it had all happened, us boys from the *Milne* all stood up. We could see Poles, Brits, Americans and Canadians throwing punches at each other, and I ducked quickly as a chair was flung in my direction. Within seconds, the Shore Patrol were on the scene, batons drawn and ready to sort out the problem.

I suggested it might be time for us to get back to the ship.

The others did not need any persuading, and a few minutes later we were staggering along Main Street. It was only as the fresh air hit us that we all realized we were very drunk.

How we actually got back to the ship, I could never quite remember, but no sooner were we on board than some of those I was with were immediately led off to the 'Tiller Flat' to sober up and sleep off the alcohol. The Tiller Flat was the hatch at the stern of the ship under which the hawsers and wire ropes were stored. Anyone able to walk up the gangway unaided was allowed to return to their mess deck, but if you could not, or were in any way obstreperous, then it was a night in the 'Tiller Flat' for you.

The next morning, waking up in my bunk with surprisingly little hangover but with the taste of stale booze on my breath, I waited for the return of my friends who had been unsuccessful in their attempts at walking a straight line the previous evening and were now locked up in the 'Flats'. I smiled to myself at having avoided that particular inconvenience.

Later that day, as I watched the second group set off for their run ashore, I knew I would be locking some of them up in the

'Flats' myself when they returned. I did not know whether to feel envious about not being able to go along with them, or, as my head throbbed and a feeling of nausea rose within me, relieved I was staying on board.

The following evening at 2200 hours, the *Milne*, along with the other ships forming Force 'H', set off eastwards in convoy through the Strait of Gibraltar, ready to face whatever the enemy would throw at us.

For now the fun was over.

* * *

Finishing my morning watch, I stood on the deck and looked out at the huge invasion force steaming towards North Africa. Operation Torch was to be a three-pronged attack, with units landing simultaneously along the coastlines of Morocco and Algeria. The western task force was to hit the area around Casablanca; the centre task force, the port of Oran; and the eastern task force was to attack the port of Algiers. Force 'H', of which HMS *Milne* was a part, was to provide protection for the landing forces from Italian submarine and U-boat attack on the approaches to the landing zones in the east.

Stretching out to the horizon were around 400 ships, formed into three convoys, ferrying soldiers and equipment from America and Britain. The hot Mediterranean sun reflected back off the steel hulls as they journeyed from their staging points, the smoke from their funnels rising high into the sky. Some ships had come directly from Britain, whilst others had only to travel the short distance from Gibraltar. This was to be the first major combined combat operation of the war involving American and British troops, and every effort had been put out to make it a success. The majority of the enemy would be the soldiers of the Vichy French government, and it was uncertain just how much of a fight they would put up, if any at all, or whether they would simply put down their weapons and join the Allies and their com-patriots in the Free French. There was so much as yet unknown.

Those with hangovers from the run ashore a day or so ago had now fully recovered, and my friends and I were starting to enjoy the sunshine and warm sea air once more. After a while, the ships started to break off and head to our pre-arranged destinations.

The threat from beneath the surface was ever present, the crew all aware that at any time a torpedo could come hurtling towards us. This peril never seemed to be absent whenever I went to sea.

A short distance across the water were other ships assigned to Force 'H', including two other 'M' class destroyers, HMS *Martin* and HMS *Meteor*, along with the battle cruisers HMS *Hermione*, HMS *Duke Of York* and HMS *Nelson*. Observing the might of the forces assembled, I feared for those about to oppose us. I thought back to the days of the Blitz and how the country was very much in danger of losing the war before it had really got going. But now both the Soviet Union and the United States were fighting with us against the Germans, and a new sense of hope filled both those at home and the soldiers, sailors and airmen of Great Britain that this war would eventually be won.

The landings in Morocco and Algeria went very smoothly and the main objectives were taken within days, the Vichy forces surrendering without putting up much of a fight, as was hoped. The Allies (First Army) would now push eastward to link up with the British Eighth Army, effectively forcing the German Afrika Korps to fight on two fronts. Eventually, in Tunisia six months later, the Germans surrendered, and the Allies had total control of North Africa.

As the landings were taking place, the *Milne* and other ships of the screen patrolled the waters nearby, searching for submarines and acting as a presence to stop any enemy ships from interfering.

Once the troops had landed, a number of ships including the *Milne* and HMS *Martin* were ordered to return to Gibraltar.

Finishing my morning watch at around 0800 hours on 10 November, I stopped on deck for a few moments before going below for some breakfast. It was another beautiful morning, the sun shining in an almost cloudless sky and a refreshing cool breeze blowing in my face. I looked to the port side and could see HMS *Martin* sailing line abreast, powering through the calm Mediterranean water just a couple of hundred yards to port. I noticed a few sailors gathered on her deck, they too having finished their watches and about to go below to get some food and rest, just like I was. I waved my hand in greeting and a few of them waved back. Had I not known any different, I might have been persuaded this was just a pleasure cruise, a peacetime sailing, one to be enjoyed.

I stayed for a while longer, enjoying the quiet and the sunshine, and watched as some of the sailors on the *Martin* waved to me one last time before going below.

A few moments later, I noticed something strange. From across the water I heard a loud bang, and suddenly a thick black puff of smoke appeared from the *Martin*'s funnel. I watched on in horrified fascination as the *Martin* seemed to be sailing lower in the water, and then she twisted as two more loud bangs were heard from her direction. She maintained her speed of around 15 knots and, less than five minutes later, her bridge was the only part of the ship visible above the waterline.

I could see sailors in the water struggling to stay afloat. The sinking had happened so quickly that only a few had managed to make it out on to the deck, and many of those had not had time to put on life jackets, let alone launch any lifeboats. It was probable there had been no time to give the order to abandon ship. I wondered if the lads I had just been waving to had managed to get off the ship, but I realized that anyone below decks would not have stood a chance.

A few moments later HMS *Martin* was gone, sinking to the bottom of the Mediterranean as though she had never existed. All trace of her vanished from the face of the earth, and most of the crew had gone with her.

Witnessing the sinking of HMS *Martin* had a profound effect upon me. It proved to me that survival on the ocean was as much down to luck as to training and preparedness. None of those lads, young men just like me, had any chance of making it out. Some were probably asleep when it happened, and the ship would have gone before they could understand what was taking place. It showed me that conflict on the ocean is different to that on land. There is no detritus of war left behind as a reminder. There is nowhere to bury the dead, the sea takes care of that. And when the conflict is over, there is nowhere to raise a monument or to collectively mourn those who perished, save in the ports from which they sailed. The battlefield of the seas looks no different after an action has taken place; it remains just the same. The sea shrouds the horror beneath its waves, consigning it only to the memories of any unfortunate soul who may have borne witness to it.

As the familiar sound of 'action stations' blasted throughout the ship, the *Milne* steered to port to try and find the submarine that had done this and to pick up any survivors. I took one last look at the clear blue sky and the calm sea reflecting back the sun's warm rays, and sighed. Before turning back to head for the turret, where I was aware of my shipmates returning to their positions behind me, I had only one thought.

There but for the grace of God . . .

Taking a deep breath I steeled myself, then turned around and ran to take up my position at 'B' turret.

CHAPTER TEN

Rescue in the Atlantic

For the remainder of November and into December, HMS *Milne* stayed in theatre for screening and convoy duties in the western Mediterranean, protecting ships as they reinforced the armies of North Africa and also convoys going on to Malta.

My nineteenth birthday came and went, observed with the minimum of fuss in Gibraltar. A slice of corned beef and a tin of carrots made for a meagre celebratory meal (potatoes being in short supply).

Later that month, on Christmas Eve, the *Milne*, now at Mersel-Kebir on the Algerian coast, was ordered to join convoy MKF5, to escort ships returning to the Clyde in Scotland.

As Christmas Day was being celebrated back home, the *Milne* was at sea, being detached from the convoy at 1100 hours to refuel at Gibraltar, before rejoining later that day. Although we were headed back to colder climes, there was a general feeling of happiness that we were returning to home waters.

However, the feeling of comfort was short-lived as, only a couple of days into the voyage, at 0340 hours on 28 December 1942, Captain Campbell received orders to redirect. He made an announcement over the tannoy system, advising us that the *Milne* had received orders to change course and we were heading for the Atlantic. There was a convoy in trouble that needed our assistance, and we were to proceed with all haste to provide it for them. We were told to stay alert and be ready to do our duty.

The convoy Campbell was referring to was ON154. This was a large group of ships heading from Liverpool to America with a cargo of ballast and trade goods. Some of the ships would be detached to sail south and drop off goods at Freetown in Sierra Leone on the West African coast. Because of this, they would sail on a more southerly course than was normal and so lose air cover early on as they journeyed out of range of the planes from Coastal Command. Waiting for them was a large number of German submarines from the *Spitz* and *Ungestum* U-boat groups.

With the threat of air support gone, the U-boats would be able to wreak havoc among the convoy, sinking many ships with ease. An urgent message was sent to the Admiralty for assistance.

The next morning at 0730 hours, the *Meteor* reported sighting a vessel. Campbell, on the *Milne*, ordered them to proceed to investigate. Twelve minutes later, flares were seen in the sky and the *Milne* headed off in their direction.

'Every available man to the port side,' came the message over the tannoy system, and so I and the members of 'B' turret, along with many other shipmates, jumped to obey the order.

In the near distance I could see four lifeboats bobbing in the water. Quickly we dragged up cargo nets and hauled them over the side, attaching them firmly to the gunwales. We watched as the ship drew closer, the men in the lifeboats paddling furiously to get nearer to us. They looked dishevelled and highly stressed, but at the same time were mightily relieved they were being rescued from a choppy and cold sea. None was wearing uniform. These were all merchant sailors.

Eventually, the boats were alongside and the men started to scramble up the netting. As they got closer to the top, I held out my hand and hauled some of them over the gunwale and on to the safety of the deck where, now knowing they were out of immediate danger, a few collapsed against the bulwark and put their heads in their hands. Others wandered around almost in a daze as matelots handed out blankets and cups of hot tea, leading some of them inside to the mess decks.

Seeing a young boy with them, I asked him how old he was. Shivering, he told me he was fourteen years old.

For a brief second I thought back to the time I had tried to join the Navy as a boy entrant at the same age. I was not too sure now whether that would have been such a good idea. Maybe the recruiting officer and my father had done me a favour after all.

As more men climbed over the gunwale on to the safety of the ship, the *Milne*'s crew became aware these were the survivors of not one, but three merchant ships.

Sitting in the mess deck a little later, once all the men had been recovered, I spoke to one of them who was sipping gratefully at a cup of tea. I asked him which ship he had been on.

He advised me he had been on the *Baron Cochrane*, but there were many sailors rescued from two other ships, the *Lynton*

Grange and the *Zarian*. He went on to tell me the Germans had attacked them at around 9.30 the previous night, and all three ships had gone down virtually together. From what he had witnessed, it looked like the majority of the crews had managed to get off the ships before they went under.

He explained that they had been in the lifeboats all night and had been extremely relieved to see us coming to pick them up.

My respect and admiration for these men was already high, and listening to his story now enhanced it even further.

And then he told me something that shocked me. The despondent look on all the merchant sailors' faces was not purely down to the fact they had just been through a harrowing experience. Each of them we spoke to said that he needed to get on to another ship as quickly as possible. I wondered why they would be so keen to get back to sea. Surely being torpedoed by the Germans was enough to put them off setting sail ever again?

They explained to us that when a merchant ship was sunk, the surviving crew's pay stops immediately at that point. With no ship, there is no more need for a crew and therefore no obligation to pay their wages. We were also told that should any of the men decide to head for home instead, they would be faced with further problems. Some of them, without ration books and with homes in the big cities which might have been destroyed by bombing, would be returning to find no job, no house, no money and no ration book. They needed to get back on a ship pretty much whether they wanted to or not.

I was shocked and saddened to hear of this lack of support for our merchant sailors. I was horrified to learn that, despite the bravery of these men in sailing in such harsh waters with minimal protection other than that provided by the escort ships, they were treated so shabbily by their own country. It did not sit right with me at all.

(In all, HMS *Milne* rescued 143 men from the three ships en route to joining the convoy ON154.)

*   *   *

Later that day, at around 1400 hours, the *Milne* and the *Meteor* made contact with the convoy, and three hours later, set off to conduct an anti-submarine sweep. Standing on the deck, having been stood down from the turret for the time being, I watched on as the two ships turned to port and raced away from the escort. It was clear to me something must have been spotted on the Asdic, but then I noticed something in the water heading towards us.

There was no mistaking they were torpedo tracks. And there were three of them.

With my heart in my mouth I watched as the ship turned towards the tracks, reducing the target area. With a morbid fascination, my eyes fixed on them, I watched all three torpedoes pass by the port side, missing the ship by only a few yards, until they disappeared from view, falling harmlessly into the deep.

In conducting this failed attack, the U-boat had now given away its probable position. 'Action stations' sounded throughout the ship, and I rushed to my position and awaited instruction.

'There's loads of them out there,' stated the Petty Officer. 'Be ready for anything, boys.'

I turned to him and frowned. I did not say anything but I could sense a distinct feeling of nervousness in the man. An air attack could be dealt with. You could see the enemy. They were clearly visible. But the enemies that sailed beneath the water, looking for opportunities to fire their torpedoes, it was those we feared the most. 'Ready for anything' meant exactly that. Be ready to engage with any U-boats that might be forced to surface; be ready to pick up survivors from those ships that had been sunk; be ready to abandon ship should the *Milne* take a torpedo in her side.

'It's like someone shooting you in the back while you're walking away,' someone had once said, and I found the analogy to be accurate. Submarine warfare was not exactly a fair fight. However, the technology to detect them was advancing all the time, and with so many reported to be out there, there might be a good chance for a little success.

I suddenly felt a surge in the ship as she turned to port, moving quickly through the water. I assumed we had caught a signal on the Asdic and were moving to investigate. If there was a chance we could avenge those merchant sailors currently resting in the mess decks, then at least it might give them some sort of closure for what had just taken place.

As the *Milne* crashed through the waves, spraying seawater across the forward deck, our senses were on high alert. Should any of the U-boats surface then we needed to be ready to shoot at them. However, if they remained beneath the waves then the 4.7 inch guns would be of no use. It would then be up to the depth charge teams to engage them.

The ship powered on in the direction the torpedoes had come from, and after a few minutes I could hear shouting outside the turret as the depth charge teams prepared their 250lb drums, setting the timers to the depth ordered and ready to eject the charges into the sea at the given time.

And then the Petty Officer heard through his headset there had been a contact and shouted to us to prepare ourselves in case the U-boat surfaced.

The loaders opened the breech and inserted a shell into each gun. I could feel the adrenalin course through my body. This was totally different to coming under air attack and defending the ship, as we had done so many times before. This was the *Milne* attacking an enemy, the ship on the front foot for once.

Shortly after the Petty Officer's announcement we heard the distinctive splashes as the depth charges were released into the water. One after another, from both sides of the ship, they were dropped into the sea by trained sailors. After a few moments there was a series of dull thuds followed by 'whooshing' sounds as the charges exploded beneath the surface, throwing seawater high into the early evening sky. It was not that important to score a direct hit on the submarine, as the powerful hydraulic shock of a close explosion might be enough to crack the U-boat's hull, either sinking it or forcing the commander to surface, whereupon it could then be dealt with by the ship's guns if he refused to surrender.

The explosions seemed to go on forever, detonation after detonation sending the water 100ft into the air. I wondered just how a submarine could survive such an onslaught but knew it all depended on the skill of the U-boat commander in avoiding the assault, and the technique of the depth charge teams in determining the correct depth at which to set the timers on the explosives.

After a few minutes, and upon completing a full pattern of charges, the *Milne* turned around and carried out a second sweep. Once more the barrels were fired overboard by expert hands, and once more explosions ripped through the water.

The tension in the turret was palpable. We knew that the officers in the bridge above would have their binoculars glued to their faces, searching the sea for any sign of debris or a submarine forced to surface due to damage sustained on the depth charge run. In the Electronic Warfare room the lads operating the Asdic would have their eyes fixed to their screens searching for the dot that would indicate the location of the U-boat, whilst at the same time listening for the giveaway 'ping' through their headphones.

With no further sighting, after half an hour the *Milne* turned back to the convoy and we took up position on the port quarter to carry out screening duties.

With no confirmed kill, there was a little disappointment within the crew. However, although we had probably been unsuccessful in sinking the submarine, we had at least chased it away and given its commander food for thought about making another run at the convoy. In that way, we had achieved our aim in protecting the ships.

Later that evening, the *Milne* again left the convoy to investigate a possible Asdic contact, but it turned out to be a false alarm. There were no further U-boat attacks on the convoy during the night, and at noon on the following day, 30 December, the *Milne* and the *Meteor* set sail for Punta Delgada in the Azores to refuel, and to drop off the survivors we had taken from the three merchantmen.

En route to the Azores it was decided the ships should send each other wireless signals as part of a ruse to draw any U-boats away from the convoy until it had sailed out of 'wolf pack' range. Hoping the Germans were listening in, the radio operators discussed a false distress call from the merchant ship *Zarian* (which had already been sunk), in the hope of drawing the submarines to that area and away from the convoy. Whether this was successful, we had no way of knowing, but at least it was something to try and protect the ships, even after we had left them to continue on their journey to North America.

The *Milne* and *Meteor* arrived in the Azores at 1000 hours on New Year's Day, 1943, and after dropping off the survivors and refuelling, we set sail later the same afternoon. During early evening the following day, we located and picked up some shipwrecked survivors of a Belgian tanker, the *President Francqui*, which had been torpedoed some days before. We continued searching in a southerly direction for more survivors but were unable to locate any. (The remainder of the tanker's crew had been rescued by two ships of the Royal Canadian Navy.)

In the early evening of 4 January, the familiar sound of 'action stations' rang around the *Milne* once more. I looked out to sea but could not see anything. There were no ships on the horizon, no lifeboats visible in the water, and we were out of range of any German airbases. This could mean only one thing: U-boats.

I looked across as the *Meteor* shot away from the *Milne*'s side, heading out in search of what they must have picked up on their Asdic. It was not long before she was dispatching depth charges into the ocean, the explosions throwing water high into the air. A few moments later, the *Milne* set off to join the hunt, the crews at the depth charge racks ensuring the barrels were primed.

For the next few hours our two destroyers carried out eight depth charge runs in the hope of sinking the U-boat that was thought to be beneath us. However, with no sign of any debris and the signal lost on the Asdic, the hunt was called off, the U-boat having successfully evaded us.

Admitting defeat, Captain Campbell ordered the destroyers away and we set course for Scapa Flow and home, arriving just after 1000 hours on 7 January.

CHAPTER ELEVEN

JW53, an Arctic Storm

It was not long after returning to British waters that the *Milne* was called to the Tyne for a refit. This was to last until early February and so gave the crew the chance to take some well-earned leave. I took the opportunity to travel back to Essex and see my sister, Annette. After an all too brief but enjoyable visit, I had to return to the ship.

In other theatres of war things were starting to become more positive. After the success of Operation Torch, the war in North Africa was starting to go the way of the Allies, the Germans now being squeezed from the east and the west. More and more troops were being poured into the region. In the Soviet Union, the Germans were starting to retreat from the Caucasus and the battle of Stalingrad was raging, but turning in the favour of the Russians. An Allied bombing campaign had commenced on mainland Europe, and the Mediterranean was still controlled by the Royal Navy. With Malta holding out against sustained attack and convoys managing to break the siege, plans were being drawn up for the invasion of Sicily, the route into Italy, but that was still some months away. The Germans and Italians needed to be defeated on the African continent before that could happen. Convoys were still getting through from North America, providing Britain with the means to sustain the war effort, and following the success of PQ18, further convoys to Russia were going ahead. Convoy JW51B had had a major success in the Barents Sea, its escorts sinking the German destroyer *Friedrich Eckholdt*.

Upon my return to the *Milne*, I discovered the ship was to form part of the escort for the next Arctic convoy, JW53. Upon hearing the news, I frowned. It was not the place I really wanted to be going back to, especially at this time of year when the weather would be at its worst. Having spent a number of weeks in warmer climes, I would once more have to don my duffel coat and woolly hat. It being the middle of winter, I knew this would be the coldest Kola Run yet. The nights were much longer, which meant air attacks might not be as frequent as they had been on PQ18, but the ever-present U-boat threat would be enough to keep us on our toes. I also envisaged many hours on deck removing ice and snow. I was not looking forward to it.

After forming up with other escorts at Loch Ewe in north-west Scotland, the convoy set off towards Iceland. Not long after we left port, a heavy storm hit the ships, a tempest the like of which no one on board had ever experienced before.

Everything not needed was locked away in store cupboards. Cooking had become impossible. Corned beef sandwiches once again became the staple food, for both lunch and dinner. A lot of tough-looking matelots succumbed to the seasickness that they had so far escaped, and I was glad not to be plagued by it too.

Any item that was not put away, riveted or tied down was thrown around mess decks and working areas, crashing against bulkheads, doors, gantries and worst of all, people. We clung to whatever we could to stop ourselves from losing our footing and getting hurt, but accidents were unavoidable and the sick bay was full of people with a range of injuries, some of them quite serious.

It had become near impossible to rest. We tried to sleep wherever we could lay our heads. Although nausea was not something I suffered too much from, some of the lads became so ill that all they could do was lie down wherever they could find a space, uncaring or oblivious to the danger we were in, rolling about and moaning loudly as the pots, pans, random pieces of kit and other ship's paraphernalia that had not been stored away flew around them. Mess decks ran with condensation and seawater, mixed in with rotting food, broken crockery and dirty clothing sloshing about the floors and adding to the rancid stench and general discomfort. Men could not go outside to throw up, their bodies too weak to make the short journey and for fear of losing their footing and going overboard into the freezing waters of the North Sea. Instead, those matelots suffering the most vomited where they lay, and this, mixed with the other detritus, made for a very disgusting mess deck.

Despite these difficulties, we nevertheless had to work. The ship still had to make its way northward to the relative sanctuary of Iceland. Suicidal dashes across open decks to reach various parts of the ship and carry out duties became common, and I thought it a wonder nobody found themselves in the sea.

At times it seemed the sea was above the ship and not below. The mountainous waves would reach 40–50ft high and hang threateningly over us like sea monsters, before the *Milne* rose on another wave and came crashing down again into the watery valleys created by the storm. The spray covered the open decks, making them slippery and treacherous underfoot. Had anyone been unlucky enough to go overboard, then they would have been done for. There was no way the ship could pick them up.

Eventually the ships reached Iceland, but hope of the weather abating now we were in the shelter of the island were dashed. The storm continued to batter us.

The sight of over fifty ships forming up, with great difficulty due to the weather, all ready for another Kola run and all that came with it, once more greeted us, and a familiar nervous excitement was felt by the crew. However, this time we sailors knew what we were in for. Whereas PQ18 was the maiden voyage for the majority of the ship's company, with JW53 the *Milne*'s crew were all now hardened veterans and knew what to expect. Although we would all rather have been anywhere else, we approached this convoy with more confidence than we had felt only a few months earlier when we had set out on our first journey to Murmansk.

The frequency of air attack on the previous runs had not been the same as on the summer convoys, due to the limited daylight hours and inclement weather, but spring was approaching and the days were now starting to get longer once more. JW53 would not have the protection of perpetual darkness enjoyed by the previous couple of convoys. With this in mind, the escort cover for JW53 was to be as large as it had been for PQ18, and there were some familiar ships taking part, including the light cruiser HMS *Scylla*. Also, the frozen Arctic Sea would force this convoy to sail further south, bringing it within easy range of the German airbase at Banak and the naval port of Altenfjord. However, after the sinking of the *Friedrich Eckholdt*, the Kriegsmarine might be less inclined to send out surface ships to take on the might of the Royal Navy.

Rear Admiral Burnett was again the commander, but this time he was travelling on the cruiser HMS *Belfast*.

As I pondered all this, I was shocked at the violence of the storm that had not let up since we left Loch Ewe. Even here, in the somewhat sheltered Seidisfjord, the wind wailed and howled, streaking the surface with foam and throwing the ship around, even at anchor. Gale force winds seemed to hit the ship from all sides, whistling down the length of the fjord and then bouncing back at us from the sheer cliffs that flanked it. It took two attempts to attach the ship to the tanker in the middle of the fjord, the gales forcing us away, snapping the berthing wires as though they were strands of cotton. It was only when we finally had it attached that our situation improved slightly, the gales now unable to funnel between the two ships.

From the shelter of the mess deck, I looked out of the porthole. As the winds continued to howl, like a thousand wolves looking to the moon, I could see the waves rising and falling ferociously. I had never known it so bad. It was as though the ocean itself was exasperated at the violence that had taken place upon it and was doing all in its power to prevent the convoy from sailing.

But sail it would.

*   *   *

The *Milne* was to form part of the 'ocean' escort and, as flotilla leader, she was to take the lead in the anti-submarine screen.

It was not long before some of the merchant ships had to return to harbour, having been so battered by the relentless storm. Some of them were carrying trucks and tanks, and others had locomotives lashed to their decks. The weight of their cargoes, some of which became dislodged in the bad weather as they were thrown around so mercilessly, made it impossible for them to continue, and they were forced back to carry out repairs and wait for more hospitable conditions in which to sail. Two of the escort proved to be the next casualties. The cruiser HMS *Sheffield* and the aircraft carrier HMS *Dasher* were also forced to turn back when the roof of the *Sheffield*'s fore turret was ripped clean off by the winds and blown out to sea, and the *Dasher* suffered serious damage to her flight deck, rendering her incapable of putting aircraft into the sky.

However, for the rest of us, we had to endure. We would have to go on regardless, and so on 20 February 1943, with signs of the weather finally abating, an already depleted but reassembled convoy set course for Bear Island and the onward leg to the Kola Inlet and Murmansk.

For three days the convoy sailed unmolested. It was only after we had passed Jan Mayen Island that the first enemy was spotted. A long-range reconnaissance aircraft circled ahead. Since we now had no aircraft carrier escort, due to the *Dasher* having to return for repairs, there was nothing to be done; it was taken for granted that the convoy's position would be relayed back to the airbases and the U-boats operating in the area.

But what the U-boat commanders did not know was that some of the ships were now fitted with high frequency direction-finding equipment, otherwise known as 'Huff-Duff'. This kit proved invaluable, since most U-boat commanders were quite chatty and prone to sending clear messages over the airwaves about a convoy's location and size and their own ability to attack it. Those manning the 'Huff-Duff' could pick these up and were then able to roughly determine where the submarines were located, so that destroyers and anti-submarine ships could be sent out to pick them up on the Asdic, and depth charge runs could take place. Although this was used to great effect, there were no confirmed U-boat kills. But it was enough to keep them at bay and achieve the objective of 'the safe and timely arrival of the convoy', as no U-boats got close enough to the ships to attack.

It was on 25 February, when the convoy was well into the Barents Sea, that the first attack aircraft were spotted. With the sound of 'action stations' ringing in our ears, cold and weary sailors manned their positions and waited for them to come within range of the ships' guns. With the *Scylla* once again taking up a side-on defensive position, joined by the destroyer screen, all guns were brought to bear on the attacking Ju-88s.

The team in 'B' turret followed the instructions of the Petty Officer and brought the turret into position. There were fourteen attacking aircraft, each carrying four 250lb bombs, coming in to conduct shallow dive-bombing runs. The order was given to fire, and the chilled air was almost instantly filled with flak and tracer shells, the escort ships putting up a fierce aerial barrage.

The attack did not last long, the airmen being clearly daunted by the prospect of having to fly through this maelstrom, with the risk of either a fiery death if hit, or freezing in the waters of the Barents Sea if forced to ditch. Dropping their bombs harmlessly away from any of the ships, they turned around and fled back to their base.

The following day, as the ships got ever closer to the Kola Inlet, eleven Ju-88s mounted an attack, their numbers no doubt depleted by their unsuccessful foray the day before. Once again, not wishing to run through the barrage, the nervous pilots dropped their payloads short and turned back.

Although the ships were now close to our destination, the danger was by no means over. We knew that this was possibly the most perilous part of the voyage. If the Germans were unsure of our exact position during the journey, they knew exactly where to find us at the end of it.

They knew that the ultimate destination was Murmansk and the ships had to enter the Kola Inlet in order to get there. 'Wolf pack' attacks were common near the Inlet as they gathered in numbers to pounce on the convoys when they sailed through. But with Asdic and the new 'Huff-Duff' equipment now in service, there was confidence the escorts could chase away any U-boats hoping to engage with the convoy.

Now that the convoy was in sight of Polyarny, at the mouth of the Inlet, we were joined by Russian ships who would escort it the rest of the way to Murmansk. The destroyers were now able to return home, picking up the returning convoy RA53.

As I watched the merchant ships sail on, I was struck again by the resilience and courage of their crews. For all the hardships they suffered, they still returned on these journeys time and time again. Even if their ships were sunk and they were rescued, they would find another berth and uncomplainingly come back to do the Kola run once more. And when they arrived at the docks in Murmansk, they came under constant aerial attack by the Luftwaffe. They were never really out of danger.

And the weather conditions on this run had been the worst I had endured. I had never known storms or weather like it. Although my time swimming in the North Sea as a child in Berwick had hardened me to cold weather, this was something else. As we sailed back towards Iceland, my mates and I were called upon numerous times to go out in the freezing temperatures to break ice off the ship. Temperatures as cold as minus 30° centigrade had to be endured to ensure the ship could progress through the water safely.

As I brushed a huge lump of ice over the side, to splash heavily into the ice-cold waters of the Barents Sea, I thought to myself of the Mediterranean. Okay, the Med had not exactly been easy, but if you have to endure difficult times, it was surely better doing it with the sun on your back, rather than an icy wind blowing snow and sleet into your face.

With the arrival of the local escort, and running low on fuel, Captain Campbell was free to take the *Milne* and other destroyers to Seidisfjord in search of diesel. However, we had not gone far when we received an SOS indicating the SS *Richard Bland* was in serious trouble. Having quickly refuelled at Akureyri on the north coast of Iceland, we set out to search for stragglers who had been blown off course during the horrendous weather. Upon arrival at the location where the *Richard Bland* had been hit, we found two destroyers, HMS *Impulsive* and HMS *Eclipse*, attempting to pick up survivors. Some of the men were in overcrowded lifeboats whilst others clung on desperately to the sides, their bodies submerged in the water. The remaining survivors were taken on board the ships, and we were able then to turn and head for the sanctuary of port and hopefully to escape from the worst of the weather.

The *Milne* left RA53 on 10 March, returning to Scapa Flow, where we were then transferred to Plymouth Command, supporting convoys on the Western Approaches for the next few months. That summer, she was nominated for a refit, and on 7 August 1943 we arrived in Hull to have it carried out, allowing the crew to take some much needed leave.

CHAPTER TWELVE

A Change of Ship

Upon the *Milne's* arrival in Hull I found out I had been selected to attend a Second Class Higher Gunnery Rate course at Chatham Gunnery School and was to leave the ship in September.

I was pleased the Navy thought I had the aptitude to take my career to the next level, but at the same time I was very sad to be leaving what had been a happy ship. Although I had been in constant danger, I knew the time I had spent on board had been the making of me. I had turned from a green recruit to a naval veteran and knew I had become a confident and capable seaman, as well as an expert turret trainer. Throughout all the *Milne's* adventures, I had not once been found wanting.

But there was no denying the last few months had been difficult. Along with my mates I had endured Arctic storms, fought off the Luftwaffe, thwarted U-boat attacks and witnessed the sinking of merchant and naval vessels. I had personally witnessed, up close, the deaths of many sailors, men just like me, something that would stay with me forever.

I was well aware I had been lucky in my life, dodging Death's scythe on many occasion. From the diphtheria epidemic as a child, to surviving the Blitz and avoiding torpedoes both in the Mediterranean and also the Atlantic, I had managed to somehow find a way through it all. Was there a guardian angel watching over me? Was it fate? Or was it just down to simple luck?

Leaving HMS *Milne* after only fourteen months was not what I had expected. There was no denying she was an excellent ship, with good officers and a captain I considered to be brilliant and fair to his men. And so it was with something of a heavy heart that I collected my rail warrant from one of the writers and set off to the train station, my haversack and hammock over my shoulder. I had said my goodbyes to Robbo and the rest of my friends and promised to keep in touch. There was a bond between us all that had been formed on the harsh waters of the Arctic and Atlantic Ocean, as well as in the North and Mediterranean Sea. It was a bond that could only really be understood by the men who had been there, and it would remain with us until our dying days.

I found Chatham pretty much as I had left it a year and a half ago and enjoyed the many weeks I spent there. It was a good break from the intensity of being aboard a warship, and I was able to relax and reflect on what I had achieved since joining the Navy. There were many other courses taking place, and I found the Higher Gunnery Rate course both exciting and interesting. The experience I had gained on active service, and the knowledge and confidence that brought, assisted me greatly and gave me a good understanding of the course content. Once I was qualified I would be posted to a cruiser or destroyer, where I would be assisting in the direction of the ship's guns, not cooped up in a gun turret. From my position in the director I would be above the ship's bridge and able to identify targets, designate them to gun crews and direct their fire. The only problem with this was that most German ships targeted the director deck when concentrating their fire during naval battles.

It was a big opportunity for me, and I found the work and responsibility it brought well within my capabilities. I had wanted to join the Royal Navy since boyhood, and it was proving to be all I had hoped it would. I was in my element. I just trusted my next posting would bring sunnier locations, without the need to chip ice off decks in freezing temperatures. But then I knew that wherever they sent me, I would go. It was all part of being a sailor in the Royal Navy.

The training involved how to instruct crews on the loading and drill for naval guns of up to 8-inch calibre. I again made use of the 'yaw, pitch and roll' machine, on which I was required to carry out a shoot with the target showing on a moving screen. The next task was how to use the power of command, and I learned how to drill squads on the parade ground at the Royal Naval Barracks (Chatham) at HMS *Pembroke*. On one occasion I was made to wait until the squad I was drilling had marched to the very far end of the parade ground before the officer gave me permission to turn them about. Having had previous experience with parade ground drill when a youngster, as part of Max Karo's army, I was confident in my approach, and the ratings I was instructing listened intently and adhered to my orders. This would serve me well in instructing turret crews when I returned to sea.

Passing the three month course with relative ease, I found I was to be posted to the 'S' Class destroyer, HMS *Savage*. Although successfully completing the course did not bring about a promotion, I was able to wear the 'cross guns' badge on my sleeve which gave me the necessary authority I required to conduct my duties, albeit without the rank.

The day I finished the course I went to see the Petty Officer writer, who handed me a travel warrant. He told me I was to join HMS *Savage* but I should first report to the Destroyer Depot Ship HMS *Tyne* at Scapa Flow. That was where the *Savage* was currently docked. He handed me the warrant and wished me a safe trip.

I put the warrant in my pocket, picked up my hammock and the small suitcase that contained all my belongings and headed for the train station. I would need to make for Thurso at the very tip of Scotland and get the ferry across to Scapa. I sighed. This would take forever. It was nearly 700 miles away! Knowing I was only 40 miles or so from Westcliff-on-Sea, where my sister Annette now lived, I thought the Navy might have allowed me some leave before joining my new ship. Alas, this was not to be, and so I prepared myself for the long journey.

As I stood on the platform I turned my collar up to the cold breeze that blew across the station. I smiled to myself as I realized almost a year had passed since the last time I had been on the Kola Run. Now that *was* cold, I thought. A Kent winter was nothing compared to what I had experienced on JW53. This kind of cold I could cope with.

It was now early February 1944, and the war was going the way of the Allies. The Germans were being forced back in Russia, having been heavily defeated at Stalingrad. The Nazis were now on their own in Italy after their closest allies had switched sides following the invasion, and were being forced to retreat from American and British forces. A sustained bombing campaign was underway against targets in Germany, and the invasion of France was thought to be coming ever closer. The Germans were very much losing the war. But I knew the fighting was far from over.

A train pulled into the station and I got on. It was carrying troops from all services and included the uniforms of servicemen from other countries. Sailors, airmen and soldiers from Britain, Canada and America, and others with flags on their arms from countries I did not know, were all mixing together, smoking, playing cards and killing time as the train trundled on. It was packed, with every seat taken. I had no intention of standing up for any length of time as my journey was likely to take a couple of days. I spotted a luggage rack in one of the compartments and, being only five feet four, hoisted myself into it. This was where I would sleep. Sometimes being of diminutive size came in handy.

For the next two days, which included numerous stops along the way, I travelled the length of England, crossing the border into Scotland where the train took me ever north towards Thurso. At one point I passed close to Berwick and was taken back to the happy childhood I had spent there, which now seemed so long ago. It had been a wonderful time, and I vowed to myself I would go back there one day, if only to visit those places that held such happy memories.

Eventually, arriving in Thurso in the early morning, I walked to the ferry terminal. I was exhausted. My body ached, having been cooped up in such a confined space for so many hours. There were many others wanting to get to Orkney, and I had to queue up and wait my turn to cross the straits.

Eventually, after a wait of a few hours, my turn came and I boarded the small ferry with a number of other sailors. I was surprised to see a couple of Wrens on board too. Eventually, we set off across an increasingly choppy sea.

Seeing a young matelot leaning against the gunwale, looking rather pale, I walked over to him and asked him if he was all right. The young sailor looked back at me, but before he had chance to reply, he turned away and vomited over the side.

Chuckling, I patted him on the back and asked if he was new to the Navy, which he told me he was, and this was his first posting. I reassured him that he would be fine and would soon get his sea legs.

I could hear laughter behind me and when I turned, I saw the two Wrens were looking in our direction and giggling, clearly finding the sight of a sailor with seasickness ironically comical.

'Aww, bless,' said one of them.

I smiled at them. The comedy of the situation was not lost on me.

A while later, the ferry docked at Lyness destroyer base and we all got off. After asking directions to HMS *Tyne*, I finally arrived at my destination. Once on board I made my way to the administration deck and approached a desk, where an experienced looking Chief Petty Officer sat with a younger rating. There was a lot of paperwork on the desk that the rating seemed to be absorbed in.

Dropping my case and hammock at my feet, I said, 'Good afternoon, Chief. Able Seaman Erswell reporting for duty. I've been assigned to the *Savage*.'

Looking me up and down, the Chief Petty Officer responded, 'HMS *Savage*, you say?'

'That's right, Chief. The *Savage*.'

'Dear, oh dear,' he replied. 'You're a bit out of luck, young man.'

I felt my heart sink. 'How so?'

'The *Savage* set sail for Hull a couple of hours ago. She's gone for repairs. You've missed it.'

'You're joking,' I said, exasperated.

'This is the Royal Navy,' said the Chief Petty Officer seriously. 'There's no jokers in the Navy, lad.'

'I'm not so sure about that, Chief,' I replied, humourlessly. 'What am I to do?'

'Looks like you'll need a travel warrant to Hull, I suppose.' Then he said, more sympathetically, 'Get yourself some grub and some rest, lad. Then you'd better chase after your new ship.'

Again I sighed. What a farce, I thought. If the Admiralty knew the ship was going to Hull then why didn't they just send me to Hull to meet it? Instead, I had spent days stuck in an overcrowded, stuffy train trundling up the length of the country for no good reason.

After having a meal and crossing back to Thurso, I caught a train to Hull arriving at around three o'clock in the afternoon. I had been travelling now for three days, and the sight of my new ship was an extremely welcome one. I walked up the destroyer's gangplank and found the administration officer, who passed me on to the coxswain.

'Erswell, Erswell, Erswell,' muttered the coxswain under his breath as he searched through the paperwork on his desk. Eventually, he pulled out a sheet and held it up, placing it on top of the pile. 'Ah yes, here you are. You've been assigned to Red Watch. That's good for you. You're in luck.'

'How so?' I asked, intrigued.

'Red Watch have just been given a week's leave. As soon as you're ready, you can go on leave, too. Where, should I make out the travel warrant to?'

I did not know whether to laugh or cry. 'Westcliff-on-Sea, I suppose.'

'Bloody hell,' said the coxswain. 'Don't get too excited about it. You're going on leave, pal.'

Westcliff-on-Sea was around 40 miles from my original start point of Chatham. By the time I got there I would have been travelling for over four days, covering a distance of around 1,500 miles, sitting in cramped trains and sleeping in luggage racks. By contrast, Chatham to Westcliff would have taken a couple of hours at the very most.

Taking the travel warrant from the coxswain, I bade him goodbye and set off on the next leg of my epic trek.

CHAPTER THIRTEEN

Another Kola Run

A week later, I returned, refreshed, to take up my new position on HMS *Savage*. I hoped that like the *Milne*, my new ship
would prove to be a happy one.

Captained by Commander Michael Meyrick, HMS *Savage*
had not long returned from convoys to Russia and had taken
part in the Battle of the North Cape on Boxing Day 1943, when
along with HMS *Duke of York*, HMS *Saumarez*, HMS *Scorpion* and
the Norwegian destroyer *Stord*, she had sunk the German battleship *Scharnhorst*. The German ship went down with the loss
of 1,932 men. Only thirty-six survivors were picked up.

The Battle of the North Cape effectively ended all Kriegsmarine
surface operations against the Arctic convoys for the remainder
of the war.

It did not come as much of a surprise to me that HMS *Savage*
was to form part of the escort for yet another Russian convoy.
The ironic thing was that my previous ship, HMS *Milne*, although
taking part in a couple more Kola runs since I had left, had now
been moved to operations in the Mediterranean. Had I stayed
with the *Milne* I would now be heading out to a sunny location instead of once more being subjected to the harsh weather
of the Arctic Ocean and all the hardships that came with it.

On 16 February 1944 I set sail for the first time on HMS *Savage*
on Home Fleet duties; six days later, we joined the ocean escort
for convoy JW57 to Russia. This was a huge convoy of forty-two
ships plus escorts, the largest ever to set sail on the Kola Run.
With the success of the previous few journeys, there was now
a huge effort to get as many supplies to the Russians as possible, to assist them in making good the superiority they were
achieving on the Eastern Front. Close escort by many destroyers, combined with air support, was proving to be effective in
repelling the U-boat threat, and with the Luftwaffe having had
little success against the convoys recently, confidence was felt
that JW57 could reach Murmansk relatively unmolested.

For myself, it felt slightly odd not joining a team in one of the gun turrets; but from my position in the director, above the bridge, I had an overall view of the ship, her guns and any enemy aircraft or ships that might appear. I settled quickly into the routine and had made a friend in Red Watch's range finder, Ratcliffe.

'Just call me "Rats",' Ratcliffe had told me when we first met. 'Everyone calls me Rats . . . no idea why!'

I took an instant liking to the man. He had a sense of humour akin to my own and always had a funny quip or joke to hand. I had no idea where he got his jokes from, but the man seemed to have an endless supply, and sometimes I found it hard to concentrate on my duties, he made me laugh so much.

Rats would pass information to the gun turrets through a linked microphone system, by which the Petty Officers in charge would then relay the messages to their teams. Whilst we were at sea we would often practise our drills to ensure we were ready for action should the enemy show themselves.

On 22 February HMS *Savage*, along with other destroyers of the ocean escort, joined the convoy. I was happy to see that, unlike the last convoy I had sailed on, when the aircraft carrier HMS *Dasher* had been forced to return after damaging its flight deck, a fully functioning aircraft carrier, HMS *Chaser*, was to accompany us on the journey. I was aware just how effective air support could be, after the success of PQ18, when the Fairey Swordfish biplanes and Sea Hurricanes had worked so tirelessly and effectively to ensure a safe passage for the majority of the ships.

Despite the fact the *Scharnhorst* was now out of action and the German High Command were reluctant to commit their surface ships against the firepower of the Royal Navy, I knew from experience that the main threat lay below the surface. There was no doubting the Germans were losing the war, but their U-boat 'wolf packs' were still very much active, as were the air bases in Northern Norway. The last time I had sailed in these waters the weather had been the biggest danger, and that had been at the same time of year as this convoy. I was pleased that this time the gales and hurricanes I had experienced on JW53 were nowhere to be seen, the sea being relatively calm. With air support and an escort of many destroyers, frigates and anti-submarine vessels, I felt confident the convoy could achieve its aim of getting the cargoes to Russia safely and in good time.

One night, when Red Watch's director team had relieved the off-going watch at midnight, Rats, seated in his position behind me, keyed his microphone and spoke to Fire Control, telling them that Red Watch were all present and correct and reporting for duty.

After receiving the acknowledgement, he asked me if I had heard the one about the farmer's three daughters.

I did not turn around but instantly smiled. I told him that I hadn't.

He then proceeded to tell me, in a very comical way, an extremely coarse joke, which had me chuckling as he told it. The way he could entertain us in his own indomitable style was always something we looked forward to when we were to go on watch. Rats was always able to keep our spirits up even during the darkest time, and all of Red Watch appreciated him for it.

And then he reached his quite vulgar punch line.

After a brief pause, the silence was broken by huge guffaws all around the ship. In fact, when I looked to the bridge, I could see the officers inside all chuckling. Surely it was too much of a coincidence for them all to be telling jokes at the same time, I thought. I turned around to see Rats, his face white, frantically flicking the switch on his microphone.

And now I really laughed. The man had forgotten to turn his mic off when he was telling the joke, and everyone had heard it, including the officers on the bridge. It appeared that, upon hearing Rats about to tell his joke, the officer in Fire Control had flicked the switch so all the ship's company could enjoy it, including the bridge, where the Captain was on duty.

Once the laughter had died down, a voice crackled through the tannoy. It was the executive officer. 'Can Leading Seaman Ratcliffe please report to Captain Meyrick on completion of his shift?'

* * *

A day after joining JW57, the familiar shape of an enemy long-range reconnaissance aircraft was spotted on the horizon. This was a four-engined Focke-Wulf Condor. To me, this was to be expected and part of a kind of routine for Arctic convoy duties. Martland aircraft were quickly scrambled from HMS *Chaser*, and the German plane promptly turned tail and headed for home. However, with the convoy's location now known, I fully expected a squadron of He-111s or Ju-88s to make an appearance not long after. However, no aircraft showed themselves and the convoy carried on.

The following day, 24 February, U-boats were detected on Asdic and some ships set out to make contact with them, supported by Swordfish from the carrier. The submarines proved to be very disorganized and unable to break through the screen to get at the merchant ships. Late in the afternoon, debris could be seen in the water after an attack by Swordfish aircraft and HMS *Keppel*, who had spotted a U-boat on the port side of the convoy. This was later confirmed as *U713*, which was sunk with all hands.

The exhilaration of sinking a U-boat was short-lived, as the very next day, having had no joy in breaking through the screen to attack the cargo ships, the 'wolf pack' turned its attention to the escorts. This was not before a supporting Catalina aircraft from 210 Squadron based at Sullom Voe in the Shetland Islands had found and sunk another U-boat, the *U601*, which went to the ocean floor taking all its fifty-one crew with it.

That night, at around 2055 hours, in a blinding snowstorm and a heavy swell, HMS *Mahratta*, one of the destroyers sailing in the stern sector of the convoy, was hit by two 'Gnat' torpedoes fired from the U-boat *U990* and sank within minutes. Despite a quick response from HMS *Impulsive* in hurrying to the ship's aid, out of her crew of 236 only sixteen survivors were rescued, frozen and distraught, from the icy waters.

The sinking of the *Mahratta* was felt by all the destroyer crews. We all knew it could quite easily have been any one of us. Although the merchant ships were being successfully protected, with the Germans now targeting the naval vessels in frustration, nobody was in any way safe.

The convoy steamed on, the crews in a constant state of alert. When on deck, all eyes looked out to the sea beyond the convoy, looking for the tracks of incoming torpedoes or a periscope that would give away a U-boat's position. Thankfully, the ships closed in on the Kola Inlet without further attack, and all merchant ships arrived at Murmansk without any of them being damaged. This was probably the most successful convoy yet, but the sinking of the *Mahratta* took away any cause for celebration, and it felt like a hollow victory.

The weather was as bad as ever. Snow squalls and gales would blow up out of nowhere, and once again I found myself on deck in the freezing cold, chipping away at ice and brushing snow over the side. It was a duty I had now come to expect and accept on the Arctic runs. There was no point in moaning about it, it was work that had to be done. I had no time to get down about it; I was always busy and had Rats to keep my spirits up if ever I felt low.

Knowing the U-boats were likely to be waiting just off the Kola Inlet for any returning ships, a new course was set for convoy RA57. This took us further east before swinging round in a large arc and then heading westward towards Bear Island and home, in the hope of shaking off the 'wolf packs', who were now happy to hit any target they could set their sights on.

For two days this tactic worked, before 'action stations' sounded on all the ships as a group of submarines was spotted on the surface, just south of Bear Island. The speed of the Swordfish pilots in taking to the air meant they were able to engage with the U-boats before they had a chance to get away, and consequently one of them, *U472*, was sunk by the aircraft. However, *U703* managed to fire a torpedo into the merchant ship *Empire Tourist*, which sank, but only after all her crew had been safely evacuated. Over the next two days two further U-boats were sent to the bottom of the sea, the *U366* by Swordfish aircraft, and *U973* having been engaged by HMS *Onslaught*, with Swordfish support.

For all their efforts at stopping the largest convoy to take to the sea on the Kola Run, the Germans had failed miserably. They had succeeded only in sinking one escort ship (HMS *Mahratta*) and an empty returning merchantman, for the loss of five U-boats. It was clear the war in the Arctic Ocean was now being won by the Allies. Ever since the success of PQ18 the Germans had been on the back foot, and this latest convoy, a total of forty-two merchant ships successfully transporting thousands of tons of cargo to Russia, had proved something of an embarrassing failure for them.

On returning to safe waters on 8 March 1944, HMS *Savage* was detached from the convoy, and two weeks later she was taken to Immingham for a refit and boiler clean.

CHAPTER FOURTEEN

'What kind of sailors are you anyway?'

Immingham Docks, across the River Humber to the south of Hull, was not my idea of a good location for rest and relaxation. The opposite watch had been granted leave, but Red Watch were made to stay on duty, having enjoyed some leave the previous time we had been in dock. However, after our duties were completed for the day, we were allowed to spend the rest of the time away from the ship.

One afternoon, whilst I was enjoying some hot food in the mess, Rats approached me and asked how I was at dancing. I told him enthusiastically that I loved to dance and wondered why he was asking me. He told me he had a soldier friend who was stationed nearby and had been invited along to a dance at the local hall that night. He thought I might like to go along with him.

I was thrilled to be asked to go and jumped at the chance. I had become a keen and competent dancer, having been used by my sister Annette to practise with when younger.

Later that evening, once we had been stood down from our duties, Rats and I, along with another friend, headed out to the hall and on arrival found it was full of soldiers and Army girls. A band played the latest tunes on a stage at the back, and some were already dancing.

After getting a drink and chatting for a few minutes, I looked around the room for a suitable dance partner. Being of small stature, I needed someone of similar height and I immediately spied a small, attractive girl in Army uniform sitting alone and tapping her feet to the rhythm of the beat. Whether she was waiting for her friends, or they were already up dancing, I did not know, but my confidence in my own dancing abilities gave me the courage to ask her to accompany me on the floor.

Handing my glass to Rats, and not giving him a chance to ask what I was doing, I strode over to the girl and stood before her.

Displaying a confidence I was not altogether feeling, I introduced myself and asked her if she would like to dance.

She looked up at me and smiled. She really was very pretty, I thought, and I held out my hand. To my absolute delight, she took it and replied that she would very much like to dance with me. There was a slight twang to her accent which I could not place, and once we were on the dance floor, I asked her about it.

She told me her name was Teresa White, but her friends called her 'Tish'. She was from Wales and was part of the anti-aircraft battery close by, although she had not been in the Army that long. As we moved to the music, it became clear that we were very well suited, immediately enjoying each other's company.

We spent the rest of the evening dancing and talking. I told her about my childhood in Berwick and how I had joined the Navy. I did not go into too much detail about what I had seen and experienced, preferring to listen to her story, which I found fascinating. The more I danced with her and looked at her, the more attracted to her I became. She really was a lovely girl, full of life and fun, with a pretty face and a pleasant demeanour.

As the night drew to a close, I realized I had not spoken to my friends since I had asked Tish to dance with me. I looked around the room for them but they were nowhere to be seen. I shrugged. Perhaps they had seen me enjoying myself and left me to it.

As the last dance was played and people started to leave the hall, I knew I could not leave it at that. I was taken with the girl and did not want this to be a one-off. As I helped her into her coat I asked what she was doing the following day and was pleased to hear that she finished her duty at 1700 hours, just as I did.

We agreed to meet up the next evening and, once we had finished work, we met in a nearby pub. It was clear to me she was very popular with her comrades, some in the pub waving to her and exchanging pleasantries, but leaving us both alone at our table to enjoy each other's company. I learned she was from a small town in North Wales, and she confided in me she had grown up with a boy who was now serving in India with the Army. Both families expected them to marry eventually, but they had not been in touch for nearly three years, and she presumed this was just something that had fizzled out. Although I told her it was very sad, I was secretly pleased to hear it.

With HMS *Savage* due to sail the following day, we exchanged addresses (mine being a PO box number) and agreed to write to each other. It was with heavy hearts that we parted company at the end of the evening, neither of us wanting it to end, knowing we would probably be apart for some considerable time.

When the ship set sail the next morning, heading out with other destroyers to escort the aircraft carriers HMS *Furious* and HMS *Searcher* whilst they conducted air strikes against German convoys off Kristiansund North in Norway, for the first time I realized I did not want to go. I had met a girl I liked, and our time together had been cut all too short. I wanted to spend more time with her, and not being allowed to do so annoyed me. The war was beginning to get in the way of other things I wanted to do with my life, and the sooner it was all over the better.

But as I thought this, I realized the war could not last much longer. The Germans were suffering heavy defeats in Russia and Italy, and the Japanese were on the back foot in the Far East. There was a distinct buzz in Britain that an invasion of mainland Europe was not far away, and once that occurred, the end would be in sight. The number of American troops being assembled in the southern counties making ready for a probable invasion was easy to see. What other reason could they be there for?

Watching the planes take off from the carriers' flight decks to conduct their air strikes, I was filled with a renewed hope the war would be over very soon. Then, maybe, life could return to some kind of normality, where people could be happy and free to do more enjoyable things once more, without the fear of death and heartache in their lives.

But I knew there was still a long way to go before that could become a reality, and until such time, I just had to get on with it.

Once the operations in Kristiansund were completed, HMS *Savage* was ordered to leave Scapa Flow and proceed to the English Channel to await further orders. By now I had been promoted to Leading Seaman (informally known as a 'killick'), and to me and the rest of the crew, there was a feeling that this was it. The invasion must be imminent, there was no other reason for it. The convoys to Russia had been suspended, not only due to the perpetual daylight the summer months brought in that theatre of war, but also because many ships were needed for something else.

Something infinitely bigger.

*   *   *

Arriving at Eastbourne on a bright summer's day in the first week of June, the *Savage* was to be deployed on patrolling duties along the south coast. However, before any orders came through, we stood at anchor just off the seaside town, well within sight of the beaches on which groups of civilians could be seen enjoying some leisure time. With little to do other than await orders and sit on deck, the men gazed in frustration at those on dry land able to enjoy the sunshine and the chance of a beer or two.

Feeling frustrated at the lack of activity, I asked the Chief Petty Officer, who was leaning against the bulkhead smoking a cigarette, if there was any possibility of a run ashore. He half laughed at my cheek, advising me that I knew full well there was no leave allowed as we were on four hours' steaming notice and I would just have to grin and bear it.

I sighed. I was bored. With nothing to do other than re-read the letters I had received from Tish, something I had done many times already, I was getting a little anxious to be doing something. I looked out at the clear blue sea and how warm, calm and inviting it looked. Not quite up to Mediterranean standards, but a million miles from the cold of the Arctic. I had a strong urge to be on it.

After a few minutes I tried my luck again. I asked the Chief if there was any chance that I and a couple of other lads could take out one of the lifeboats that hung at the port side of the ship. I attempted to persuade him that it would give us a chance to practise our basic sailing skills, something we had not done for quite a while. One or two others listened in to the evolving conversation with interest.

The Chief drew on the last of his cigarette and threw the butt over the side. He paused for a moment, which I took to mean he was contemplating the idea. One of my pals, Joe, a Leading Hand who was sitting alongside me, decided to press the advantage. He argued that it would boost morale and that if we stayed close to the ship then we could be back on board in no time at all. He said he had done a bit of sailing as a youngster as well as in the Navy, and we knew what we were doing.

In the end, the Chief relented and agreed to speak to the Captain to see if permission could be granted. He walked away towards the bridge and after a few minutes he returned. It was good news.

The Captain had granted permission under the proviso that we stayed close to the ship and came back on board in double quick time should we get the signal to move. We were ordered not to stray too far, to keep our eyes on the ship for any signals and to return immediately we were ordered to.

Ten minutes later, myself, Joe and another Leading Hand named Harry had lowered the whaler into the sea, and all three of us climbed aboard. Within a few minutes we had the sail rigged and, with the aid of a stiff breeze, pulled away from the ship, Harry at the tiller. I waved at our shipmates on the deck of the *Savage* as they watched us pull away.

'See you, lads,' I called to them sarcastically. 'Don't have too much fun while we're away.'

Once we were clear of the ship we joked about heading for shore and finding a pub to spend the afternoon in. We were in very good spirits, and I took off my hat and leaned back, closing my eyes and letting the sun's rays warm my face, leaving the other two to get on with sailing the boat.

An hour later, with the wind picking up, we were nearly two miles from the ship and drifting further. Then Harry remarked he could see flags on the ship. Someone was signalling to us. It was time for us to return, and so we put the boat on the port tack.

Getting back was proving to be more difficult than we thought it would be. Despite our tacking this way and that, the ship seemed to be getting no closer. With the wind picking up and the tide turning against us, we were heading more towards land than the ship. It was becoming a struggle. We could clearly see people on the beach whistling and waving to us.

I told my two friends that we really should be better at this than we were showing ourselves to be. After all, weren't we the finest sailors in the Royal Navy? Harry reminded me that we had only had a week's seamanship training at HMS *Ganges* and this was some time ago. None of us had touched a sailboat since.

After a few more minutes of getting absolutely nowhere, we started to worry. If we were not back at the ship soon, we would be in serious trouble. We decided to put the sail away and get the oars out. Maybe we could make better progress that way. Quickly we disassembled the sail and drew out the oars. Placing them in their housings, Harry and I pulled back on them, with Joe now at the tiller.

The signals from the ship were now becoming continuous, and Joe called for us to put our backs into it, which did not go down too well with the pair of us sweating at the oars. Harry asked why the ship didn't just simply come over to pick us up, as they could see we were struggling. He was met with derision from Joe and me. We told him we couldn't see the Captain raising the anchor of a Royal Navy destroyer to collect three idiotic matelots who couldn't handle a simple sailboat. To make matters a whole lot worse, the searchlights on the *Savage* started to flash in our direction, ordering us back to ship immediately. We realized we were for the high jump once we got back on board.

After forty more minutes of pulling on the oars, I looked round and saw we had made little progress. We were all now sweating profusely and feeling totally exhausted. The absurdity of the situation was not lost on me, and I began to laugh.

'Bloody hell, lads,' I said. 'We could have invaded France, the three of us. We're halfway there already.'

This set off the other two, and as the three of us laughed, despite our worsening situation, we were initially unaware of the sound of an engine getting louder.

'Oh, you've got to be joking me,' declared Joe, looking over my shoulder.

I turned my head in the direction my friend was looking and sighed.

Approaching us was a motorized launch. What had caused Joe's consternation was, emblazoned upon its side, the roundel of the Royal Air Force. It was an RAF Search and Rescue boat.

This only set me off in fits of laughter once more. The irony was not lost on me.

As it drew closer, the coxswain of the launch, not trying to hide his amusement in any way, called out, asking if we needed any assistance. Sheepishly, Joe replied that we did and could he be so kind as to tow us back to our ship.

A line was thrown and I secured it to the bow. Without much ceremony the launch set off, dragging the whaler back through the choppy waters in the direction of the *Savage*.

Travelling at around 14 knots, each bounce on the choppy waves sent seawater cascading over the side, soaking the three of us. If I did not know any different, I could have sworn they were doing it on purpose. What convinced me was the sound of laughter from the RAF launch and the grin on the face of the coxswain sitting at the stern as he watched us bouncing across the water.

Within minutes we were pulling up alongside the *Savage*. The side of the ship was lined with sailors, all smiling and enjoying the predicament their fellow matelots had got themselves into. After unhooking the tow line, and with a sarcastic 'Cheerio' from the RAF crew, mixed with much laughter from them and those on the ship watching, the three of us drenched sailors were hauled on board, and the RAF launch sped away. There was no doubt they would have a laugh with their comrades later when telling the tale of how the RAF rescued three hapless sailors in the Channel.

As we stood before the officer of the watch we knew that we would never live this down.

'You didn't need to clear the lower decks to welcome us back,' I said to the Master-at-Arms, who was standing to the side of the officer.

'They're here to witness you hanging from the yardarm,' he stated angrily. 'Now get yourselves up to the bridge, the Captain wants to see you . . . and don't get any water on my deck!'

A minute later, the three of us were standing to attention before Captain Meyrick. Alongside my two companions, I stood in silence as he berated us.

'Don't you know you've delayed the ship from sailing?' fumed the Captain. 'Didn't you know you were on a lee shore? What kind of sailors are you anyway? Having to call out the RAF to rescue the Navy is a disgrace to the service! The next time you try to invade the French Coast on your own, I hope you succeed! You will each receive seven days' stoppage of pay. I wish I could give you more punishment than that, but as you're all Leading Seamen, you're busy enough with your working parties.'

Later, after we had changed out of our wet clothes and endured another rollicking from the Master-at-Arms, the three of us sat in the mess, where we suffered more teasing remarks from our comrades, who all seemed to think the whole thing was quite hilarious.

We bickered among ourselves about whose fault it had been. Joe had told us he had sailed before he joined the Navy, and we had assumed he was something of an expert. It turned out he had merely been on a paddle boat as a young child on the lake in his local park. We found this highly amusing and were able to laugh at what had happened now we were safely back on board.

I chuckled. 'A real Lord Nelson, you are. And who is this Lee Shaw fella, anyway, that the skipper kept ranting on about? I've never heard of him!'

We agreed the punishment of seven days' loss of pay the Captain had handed down to us was probably justified, and understood the Master-at-Arms would probably have his beady eye on us for the foreseeable future.

However, any chance of completing further punishment would have to be put to one side. More important matters would soon take over the ship's priorities.

CHAPTER FIFTEEN

The Beginning of the End

As May 1944 wore on, it was apparent a major action was to take place very shortly. The build-up of thousands of troops in the southern counties and the number of ships gathering and patrolling in the English Channel gave away that an invasion of mainland Europe was imminent. However, nobody knew exactly where it was to take place and nobody knew exactly when. Rumour and speculation abounded, but there was an acceptance that it would happen, and very soon.

However, with the ship docked in Portsmouth, three days' leave was granted to some of the crew, myself being one of them. I decided I did not want to waste a single minute of it and so bought a train ticket to Immingham to call on Tish, whose letters I had now read dozens of times. I had so much news to tell her and I could not wait to see her again.

Upon arrival at Immingham I headed for her workplace and asked to see her. A few minutes later, she was standing before me, as lovely as I remembered. She seemed as pleased to see me as I was to see her.

After we had embraced she became tearful. I asked her what the matter was, and she explained there was no way she would be allowed to spend any time with me. She was on duty for the next few days and would be unable to get any time off.

I was not happy. I had less than three days before I needed to be back in Portsmouth and I had not seen her for weeks. We had so much catching up to do. I was determined that we would spend some time together and told her that I wanted to speak to her commanding officer. I asked for her name, and once Tish had given it to me, I stepped past her and headed for the administration block.

Once there, I asked to see Tish's C.O. and was made to wait for a few minutes. Eventually, a woman in her early thirties in the uniform of a captain approached and asked me, quite sternly, what she could do for me.

I decided to maintain my composure and not to antagonize her, since showing her due respect might prove pivotal in the discussion I was about to embark upon. I had to get on her good side if I was going to achieve what I wanted.

I explained to her I had been away at sea for a number of months and hadn't had a chance to see Tish in all that time. My ship had given me a three-day pass before we set sail again for potentially another few months at sea, and this was my one chance to spend any time with her. I had travelled all the way from Portsmouth that day to see her, and she had informed me she couldn't get a single hour off to spend with me. I asked her C.O. if she could do anything to help my situation.

She advised me, as if I did not know already, that there was a war on and certain sacrifices needed to be made. The Army could not let people have time off as and when they liked, just because their boyfriends came calling.

After telling her I was well aware there was a war taking place, as I had been fighting it for the past two years, I explained I was only asking for her to give Tish a two-day pass so we could see each other, before I had to head back to that war. With it also being a weekend, I thought she might be more sympathetic.

The captain thought for a moment, and then I realized my words had struck home. She relented, saying she would grant Tish a twenty-four-hour pass and she could leave with me right away. Although this was less than I had hoped for, I did not want to push my luck and so agreed to have her back by midday the following day. I realized this was the best I was going to get. I thanked her, and after she had written out the pass, I went to tell Tish.

Tish could not believe how brazen I had been but was delighted that we could spend the rest of the day and the following morning together.

Now that we had been granted this short time together, we needed to make the most of it. I asked her how she wanted to spend it, and she told me there was a dance on at the Pier Pavilion in Cleethorpes that night and maybe we should go to that, as it was not too far away.

This was music to my ears. I loved to dance, and the happy memory of our first time together, dancing all through the evening, was still fresh in my mind. This was a perfect idea.

We made our way to Cleethorpes and booked into a boarding house. The proprietor asked no questions. This was wartime after all, and owners of guesthouses and bed and breakfast establishments would sometimes turn a blind eye to the matrimonial status of couples staying with them.

After having a nice meal and spending a few hours together, we set off to the Pavilion and enjoyed another evening dancing and chatting. I entertained her with stories of all my recent adventures. I told her of my time sailing on the convoys and the story of how my friends and I got stranded in the whaler and had to be rescued by the RAF, which she found highly amusing. I told her that although we and the rest of the crew found it quite funny, the Captain and the officers clearly did not!

The following morning, Tish and I left the boarding house and went for a walk. We wandered the area chatting and laughing. I realized this girl was having an effect upon me that no other girl thus far had had, and I was beginning to dread being parted from her.

I looked at my watch.

'Good God!' I exclaimed. 'It's nearly eleven o'clock. We need to get you back, otherwise your C.O. will have my guts for garters. I promised to have you back for twelve.'

With only an hour to go we found a quiet spot away from prying eyes behind a chapel, where we enjoyed a few minutes in each other's arms. Finally it was time to go, and with heavy hearts we approached the barrack gates, arriving there just before the deadline of midday. After one last kiss, Tish turned and walked away. I watched her as she entered the camp, not wanting to turn away and head for the train station and the long journey back to Portsmouth.

'Hey, pal,' said a soldier who was heading out of the gates. He had just passed Tish on her way in. 'What have you said to that girl? What have you done to upset her?'

'I don't know. We only said goodbye,' I replied. I, too, was distressed at the parting.

'Well, she was crying her eyes out, mate,' said the soldier, moving past me.

I sighed and turned away to walk to the station.

Upon my return to HMS *Savage*, I wrote a letter to her, telling her how much I had enjoyed our time together and that I hoped to meet up again very soon. However, history was to take a dramatic course, and I was unable to find the opportunity to write to her for some time. And then her letters to me dwindled until I was not receiving any at all. Further enquiries made with the Army some weeks later yielded no results, until eventually I had to accept the romance with Tish was over.

I assumed the soldier she had told me of had returned from India and their courtship had resumed; or perhaps she had been transferred to another unit and had lost my address. There was no other explanation for her to stop contacting me.

I would never fully understand what had happened. Teresa White had just disappeared out of my life, and I cursed the war for spoiling my future happiness.

*   *   *

4 June 1944

I stood on deck watching the torpedo teams carrying out their drills. The ship was once again at anchor after spending a couple of days patrolling our area of operations between Worthing and Dungeness. I had been given the job of bosun's mate, and piping the crew to dinner was one of my responsibilities. I waited patiently as the men worked, occasionally looking at my wristwatch until the second hand reached the correct time. After what had happened in the whaler, I did not want to get anything wrong. I watched on as the men removed the rails from the side of the ship to gain better access to the torpedoes and check their timers and rotors, and whatever else it was they needed to do. I was unsure, my own expertise being with the huge 4.7 inch guns that protruded from the turrets all along the ship.

I looked out to sea and could see a lighter passing between the ships in the harbour, dropping off mail and supplies. I observed as it turned and headed in the direction of the *Savage* and sighed. I knew I would not be getting to the mess for my own dinner until I had assisted them.

I looked again at my wristwatch and saw the second hand hit the right time, then raised the whistle to my mouth and blew, signalling it was dinner time and the men should complete what they were doing and head down to the mess decks for some food.

I watched on as they quickly tidied their work area, replaced the guardrail and hurried past me into the ship. Other teams on deck also rushed to the doorways to get to their meals and the tot of rum that awaited them, leaving me alone on deck.

I could see the lighter getting closer and so pocketed the whistle and moved to the side of the ship. They signalled to come along-side and I waved them an acknowledgement. When they were only a few feet away, I threw them a line to attach to their hawser, leaning over the guardrail as I did so.

To my total shock, the guardrail gave way, and before I could stop myself, I was tumbling over the ship's side and into the English Channel. The shock of the cold water caused me to momentarily panic, but after a second or two I composed myself and I knew I needed to get out of the water as soon as possible.

As I struggled to the surface, after first swallowing a mouth-ful of seawater, I was horrified to see I was going to be caught between the two vessels, the space between them diminishing rapidly. There was nothing the crew of the lighter could do to slow their progress towards the ship's side.

Realizing the danger I was in, of being crushed between the two vessels, I struck out towards a rope I saw dangling over the lighter's side. Upon reaching it I managed to scramble aboard the barge, helped by two of its crew, just as the lighter came up against the ship. Had I been a few seconds slower, I would have been crushed between them.

Lying on the deck, breathing deeply, soaked to the skin and with my heart thumping rapidly in my chest, I immediately understood just how close I had come once more to being killed. What a strange way for it to have happened, I thought. After all I had been through, for it to end like that, all down to someone being too eager to get to their afternoon meal and forgetting to put the locating pin in the guardrail.

The crew of the lighter were as angry about it as I was. They knew how close they had come to killing me, through no fault of their own. I told them not to worry about it, as I was unharmed. I thanked them for hauling me aboard and, once my breathing and heart rate were back to normal, I got to my feet.

A few minutes later, I was back on board ship. I headed for the guardrail, and seeing the locating pin on the deck, I hauled it into position and made the rail safe. Then I looked around and realized not a single person on board had witnessed what had taken place.

My heartbeat now back to a steady pace, I headed off to the mess deck to change out of my wet clothes and get a hot drink. This was the second time in the last week or so that I had received a soaking courtesy of the English Channel.

CHAPTER SIXTEEN

The Normandy Landings

'Have you ever seen anything like it?' said Rats, sitting behind me in the director. 'This is massive. This is history being made right now. And we're a part of it.'

I followed his gaze and looked out to sea.

By the light of a high moon I could see an armada the like of which had never been assembled before. It took me back to Operation Torch and how impressed I had been by the number of vessels amassed for the invasion of North Africa. This was on a completely different scale. For as far as I could see, there were ships of every kind: destroyers, frigates, minesweepers, troopships and landing craft, all making the journey across the English Channel to our destination of Normandy on the French coast.

The invasion should have taken place the previous day, but due to bad weather it was postponed for twenty-four hours, the commanders hoping for better conditions the following day. There had been only a three-day window for the invasion force to set sail, as the tides and moon had to be just right. Five thousand ships had been assembled in the southern English ports to convey 160,000 troops from America, Britain and the Commonwealth across the short stretch of water to finally liberate Europe from Nazi oppression. The next few days would determine if this was to be a success, a victory that should ultimately lead to the ending of the war once and for all.

HMS *Savage*'s role in Operation Overlord, as it was codenamed, was to protect the invasion force from enemy sea attack, giving it an unhindered route to the beaches. We were to patrol the area, watching for U-boat or E-boat activity and nullifying any threat these might pose. The ship was part of the Eastern task force, to the left of the armada, near to where the British and Canadians would land at Juno and Sword beaches.

As I looked out at the ships and landing craft, I felt for the men on board, whose job it was to land on those beaches and attack a German army that would no doubt fight hard to repel them. Many who were to assault the beaches were not used to sea travel, particularly in small craft that would have taken several hours to cross the Channel, and would undoubtedly be suffering from seasickness when they got there. They would have this to contend with, as well as being shot at by German machine guns.

'It's amazing,' I replied at last. 'This is magnificent. But I wouldn't like to be with those boys going ashore though, Rats. It's going to be a hard day.'

We had guessed this would be the day for the invasion. After being stood down the previous night, we had heard the sound of aircraft passing overhead in the early hours of the morning, taking paratroopers and troop gliders into France to take strategic targets prior to the main invasion. We understood that General Eisenhower, the Supreme Commander, must have given the green light for the operation to go ahead.

We sailed on, getting ever closer to the French coastline, and as the sun started to rise just before 0600 hours, I could hear the sound of heavy guns firing further to the south. The naval bombardment had started. The big guns of the Royal Navy's destroyers and cruisers, led by the light cruiser HMS *Belfast*, pounded targets on land, softening them up and hoping to make it easier for the troops about to disembark the landing craft on to the heavily fortified beaches.

As the morning wore on, the sound of battle could be distinctly heard on the ship as the Germans fought back to prevent the invasion force from gaining a bridgehead. News coming through to us was at first vague, but resistance to the south, particularly on Omaha beach, where the American Rangers had landed, was proving to be extremely fierce.

My shipmate and I knew the significance of this day. This was probably the most important action of the whole war so far. If the Allies could establish a foothold on the beaches, then more supplies and troops could be brought ashore, reinforcing those brave men who were fighting to make Overlord a success. Once an Allied army was established on French soil, with the Germans fighting a losing battle in the east against the Soviets and retreating further north in Italy, the days of the Nazis would be well and truly numbered.

HMS *Savage* continued patrolling our designated area. We had made no contact with enemy ships. This was unsurprising, due to the amount of firepower the armada possessed. Any German vessel attempting to attack us would be wiped out very quickly.

Over the next week, the news came from France that although the Germans were fighting strongly, the bridgehead was being expanded further into Normandy. The *Savage* and other ships were now called upon to escort troop and supply ships across the Channel; returning ships were also to carry the wounded from the fighting. It was clear the initial stages of Overlord had been a success and the bridgeheads were close to being linked up. However, some of the initial objectives had not yet been reached, and it would be many weeks yet until Caen, an objective on the first day, would finally fall to the British, and the invasion force could then move out deeper into France.

E-boat activity in the English Channel was becoming more common. On D-Day itself there had been a half-hearted attempt by vessels operating out of Cherbourg, to the south of the landings, where a number of E-Boats fired torpedoes from some distance away to no effect, before returning to port, no doubt realizing they could do nothing against such a huge force. However, the German fast-attack craft had now become bolder, and attacks on shipping in the Channel were becoming more frequent.

The escort ships were therefore employed to stop the E-boats having any real effect on the transport of supplies and men to support those who had landed and to ensure the success of Operation Overlord.

One such occasion was on 26 July 1944, when HMS *Savage*, along with HMS *Obedient* and HMS *Opportune*, was called into action off the coast of Dungeness to counter E-boats of the 6th German MTB Flotilla attempting an attack on shipping returning to Britain following a delivery of men and materiel to Normandy.

The small German vessels were much quicker in the water than our big destroyers, but their firepower was significantly less. As they sped along, firing their 20mm and 37mm cannon to no effect but hoping to successfully get off one of their four torpedoes, they were quickly brushed aside when the shells from our 4.7 inch guns came flying their way.

In my position in the director, assisting with co-ordination of the guns to the targets, I knew a single direct hit on an E-boat would be enough to blow it out of the water and kill everyone on board. However, as was usual during these actions, as soon as the destroyers opened up in their direction, the German boats would turn and head for home, lest one of the British shells find its target.

The E-boats proved to be a minor irritation in the whole scheme of things, and the reinforcements, munitions and other supplies crossed largely unhindered, due to the presence of the Royal Navy controlling the English Channel.

CHAPTER SEVENTEEN

Back to Russia

In August 1944 HMS *Savage* was released from Dover Command and ordered to make her way back north to rejoin the Home Fleet. Throughout August and September we were deployed to the North-West Approaches, escorting convoys entering and leaving British waters. During October the ship formed part of the screen for the light cruiser HMS *Bellona* and the new aircraft carrier HMS *Implacable* during operations in Norway, when the carrier's Fairey Firefly and Fairey Barracuda aircraft attacked the German airbases at Sorreisa and Bardufoss.

The significance of this was not lost on me. These were some of the airbases the Nazis had used when attacking the Arctic convoys I had sailed on. The fact the Royal Navy was reversing that action, that is, the ships were attacking the Luftwaffe and not the other way around, highlighted to me just how much the fortunes of war had now changed. With American and British forces advancing through France towards Germany from the west, and reports the Russians were conducting a major offensive in the east, the Nazis were now being squeezed. Just like my shipmates, I was convinced the war in Europe would soon be over.

As the year headed towards a close and the weather in the *Savage's* theatre of operations became increasingly inclement, I wondered whether I maybe should have stayed with the *Milne*. I understood my previous ship was still sailing in the Mediterranean Sea, where my old comrades, although no doubt enduring their own particular hazards, would at least be doing it in the sunshine.

In early November, HMS *Savage*, along with another 'S' Class destroyer, HMS *Scorpion*, set sail on an independent run to the Kola Inlet to deliver free Norwegian troops to Russia, for an attack on German-occupied northern Norway as part of Operation Freeman, alongside Russian troops. However, this Kola run was different to the others I had thus far taken part in. This time, we were not escorting slow-moving merchant ships and so we could travel at top speed, much too fast for any U-boats to keep up with us. With most of the Nazis' airfields in Norway now having been abandoned, and some of their planes moved to France or to the war on the Eastern front, the run went without hindrance and we arrived at the Kola Inlet on 6 November.

However, as we approached we remained constantly aware of the U-boat threat at this juncture, because the German 'wolf packs' gathered in the area, knowing all journeys to Murmansk would have to pass this point. With Asdic conditions being poor and the Germans having the new 'Gnat' torpedoes, missiles that homed in on the sound of a ship's propellers, the advantage would be with them should they decide to attack the ships as they embarked on the final leg of the journey to port.

But the British had ways to combat this threat. 'Hedgehog' and 'Squid' anti-submarine weaponry now made it possible for the Royal Navy to attack submarines from some considerable distance away, removing the need to pass directly over the target to launch depth charges. This, combined with the knowledge the war was as good as lost, and the lack of experience of some U-boat commanders and crews, was probably the reason why, despite being in the area and with targets available, the U-boats did not attack. However, this did not stop a sense of nervousness on board the *Savage*, the crew on deck keeping lookout for the signs of a periscope, snorkel or, worst of all, the track of a torpedo heading in our direction.

The one thing that had not changed, however, was the weather. Once again I found myself on deck clearing ice and snow. But many of the Norwegian troops on board were also employed in this unenviable task, somewhat alleviating that particular duty.

On 11 November, HMS *Savage* joined the convoy RA61A escorting, amongst others, the ocean liners SS *Empress of Australia* and SS *Scythia* back to Britain. These ships had returned nearly 11,000 Soviet prisoners, who had been liberated from PoW camps in Europe, back to their homeland, in order for them to take part in the coming action. The home journey would thus have to be taken at a slower pace, and we were not long out of the Kola Inlet when 'action stations' was called.

It had been a while since I had been involved in any skirmish in the Barents Sea, but the familiar conditions took me right back to the journeys I had made in the first months of my war. It was not long before the sound of an explosion was heard. The 'Captain' class frigate HMS *Mounsey* had been hit by a Gnat torpedo whilst sweeping the offshore waters of the Kola Inlet for the passage of the convoy. Although she was not sunk, she had to return to Murmansk for repairs. The U-boat concerned was subsequently chased away by patrolling anti-submarine ships, and the convoy carried on, the destroyers forming a screen to protect the rest of the convoy as they exited the inlet.

With the weather so bad, the threat of air attack was small, so it came as something of a surprise when, a day later, a Blohm & Voss BV138 reconnaissance plane was spotted in the air to the south. As it flew around the edge and out of range of the convoy, word came to the director that the bridge had sent a signal to the enemy aircraft:

'You are making us dizzy, will you go the reverse way?'

I looked to the skies, and sure enough, the German plane turned around and proceeded to circle the convoy in the opposite direction.

A few minutes later, approaching aircraft were spotted in the skies, and Grumman Wildcat fighter aircraft from the carrier HMS *Campania* were scrambled and took to the air to meet them. Seeing the strength and determination of the British aircraft heading their way, the planes dropped their bombs well short and turned to head back to base. This was not before a BV138 had been shot down.

The remainder of the voyage went without incident, and the *Savage* arrived back at Greenock on 17 November to resume duties once more with the Home Fleet.

For the remainder of the year, HMS *Savage* was involved in two operations (Urbane and Lacerate), supporting the aircraft carriers HMS *Trumpeter* and HMS *Premier* as they conducted mine-laying off the Norwegian coast between Bergen and Stavanger and air strikes against targets in Ramasund and Skatestronmen.

As my third Christmas in the Royal Navy came and went, there was now a sense the Norwegian campaign was drawing to a successful close. The Germans had started to abandon many bases in the country, sending their much needed troops to fight in other areas. News coming from the Eastern Front was that Russian forces were deep into Poland and preparing a major offensive to break into Germany itself. In the west, France had all but been liberated, but there was major fighting in the Ardennes region of Belgium as the Germans threw everything they had into a counter-attack, a last-ditch effort to push the Allies back towards the sea. If the Germans were unsuccessful, which they were likely to be, then the war could not last more than a few more months.

For myself and my colleagues on HMS *Savage*, this came as welcome news. Maybe with the Russians doing so well and the Norwegian theatre looking to come to an end, there might be less need for convoys to Russia.

The weather was by now at its most ferocious, and on New Year's Day 1945 I found myself on yet another run to the Kola Inlet on convoy JW63, escorting mainly American merchant ships. The weather was as bad as, if not worse than, on any other Russian convoy I had been involved in. Maybe this, combined with the near total darkness of each day, ensured the convoy arrived at its destination a week later without being detected by the enemy.

But as bad as the run into Murmansk had been, the return leg, convoy number RA63, was much worse. Hit by a gale of 80 knots, the sea threw the ships around on 45ft high waves, dispersing them far and wide. Huge rolling waves hit the ships, spraying spume across open decks, combining with the sleet and snow that was so common in these waters. The American Liberty ships suffered the most, some of their structures being held together by hawser lines hastily rigged by desperate crews fighting to save their ships and their very lives. To break up in weather like this meant certain death. No other ship would have the ability to come to their aid.

Along with the rest of Red Watch in the director above the bridge, I held on to the apparatus for dear life. Being so high on the ship meant the swaying of the vessel as she crashed through the water, fighting to stay on course, was felt most severely, throwing us into each other and against our equipment. To operate against an attack in any way would be nigh-on impossible, but any chance of enemy action whilst the tempest raged was highly unlikely.

By the time the cyclone had passed, to be replaced by an equally horrendous blizzard, the ships had been scattered and many were unable to be traced. To gather them back together again, the senior officer of the escort signalled the Admiralty to ask for all ships to rendezvous at Thorshavn in the Faroe Islands, to regroup and assess any damage.

In the meantime, snow and ice had to be cleared, and once again I found myself out on deck, fighting to keep my footing whilst at the same time attempting to chip the ice away and throw it into the sea. It was during these times I cursed my luck and wished I was back aboard the *Milne*, where my old friends were currently enjoying the sunshine of the Mediterranean.

Eventually the *Savage* arrived at Thorshavn on 18 January, and over the course of the next couple of days I watched as the returning ships limped into port, some worse for their experience than others. It was with a great deal of relief that every ship that had set out was accounted for. There had been no losses.

Despite the ridiculously bad weather experienced on JW63 and RA63, this was the first Russian convoy that had gone completely undetected by the Germans. There had been no enemy attacks whatsoever, but then, this was hardly surprising considering the harsh Arctic conditions we had been forced to sail under.

Whilst refuelling from a tanker anchored nearby, I looked out to the other ships waiting patiently. The thick, virtually impenetrable snowfall made it impossible to see very far, and I wondered just exactly how they would all form up for the final journey back to Britain.

It turned out this was organized by the Admiralty once more, and after a day or so at anchor waiting for some of the ships to carry out temporary repairs, the convoy once again set sail to resume its journey, with HMS *Savage* arriving back at Scapa on 21 January.

* * *

After spending the end of January and early February in Belfast undertaking a refit, HMS *Savage* took to the sea again, joining the aircraft carriers HMS *Premier* and HMS *Puncher* and the cruisers HMS *Norfolk* and HMS *Dido* in a night shipping attack off the coast of Bud, Norway, as part of Operation Selenium. This was an attempt to stop the evacuation of German troops from Norway (they had by now all but abandoned the country), by attacking German shipping, laying mines and attacking tankers bringing in fuel to supply those ships. HMS *Savage*'s role was to support the carriers and cruisers.

On 21 February, the *Savage* was detached to provide escort duties for the final leg of convoy RA64, which was returning from Murmansk after coming under sustained U-boat and air attack, the Germans trying to make up for their lack of success on previous runs. Two ships had been sunk near to the Kola Inlet when attempting to join them from Archangel, but on 17 February, at the mouth of the Kola Inlet, the corvette HMS *Alnwick Castle* and sloop HMS *Lark* sank the German U-boat *U425* with depth charges, with no survivors.

However, on the same day the Germans managed to hit the *Lark* with torpedoes; she was towed back to port but was damaged beyond repair. A further two vessels, the American merchant ship SS *Thomas Scott* and the corvette HMS *Bluebell*, were both attacked and sunk by German U-boats, the *Bluebell* going down in less than thirty seconds with only one survivor out of a crew of eighty-six.

The return convoy was carrying almost 500 Norwegian refugees from the island of Sørøya, which had come under German attack. Four destroyers had been sent by the Admiralty to pick them up, and they were distributed amongst the ships of the convoy.

As the convoy moved out of the Kola Inlet and into the wider Barents Sea, they were hit by a storm of biblical proportions, scattering the ships far and wide. Only when the weather abated a day or so later did they realize how dispersed they had become and how damaged some of the ships were. On 20 February, when most of the convoy had reassembled, some of the ships limping badly, they came under air attack from twenty-five German dive bombers from the Bardufoss airbase, still operational at the time. However, the planes were fought off without the loss of any more ships.

On 21 February 1945 HMS *Savage* reached the convoy, and the following day another gale hit, scattering the ships once more. This was one of the worst storms ever to hit the Barents Sea, and after it calmed down it was some time before the main body was able to reassemble. Due to the damage caused by the storm, a few stragglers hung back to effect temporary repairs.

The next day, whilst in the director on watch, I saw the sky again fill with German aircraft. A force of torpedo bombers was headed in our direction. Quickly the ships went to 'action stations', firing a barrage of shells into the air to force the attackers away. From where I was, at the highest point on the ship, I had full view of the action taking place. However, it was not to last long, since those aircraft that had managed to drop their torpedoes missed all the ships, and the rest turned away.

However, the Luftwaffe was not yet finished with the convoy.

The American Liberty ship SS *Henry Bacon* was struggling to keep up, having suffered major storm damage, and was now lagging some miles behind. She was a sitting duck.

The German planes attacked her for over an hour, dropping bombs and torpedoes and strafing the decks with machine gun fire. Her gunners fought back valiantly, shooting down a number of enemy aircraft and blowing up torpedoes as they headed towards the ship, before finally she was so badly damaged she had to be abandoned. Unfortunately, due to her carrying nineteen Norwegian refugees and having lost two lifeboats in the action, there was not enough room in the boats for everyone on board.

The lifeboats were crammed with as many refugees and crew as they could physically handle, and a raft was hastily constructed from ballast which took care of some more of the crew. However, as the ship was sinking some men remained stranded on board. Places in the lifeboats and on the raft were given up by older crew members to some youngsters, and eventually, as the ship sank beneath the waves, twenty-six men went down with her.

The survivors were picked up by three British destroyers, HMS *Zambezi*, HMS *Opportune* and HMS *Zelest*. None of the Norwegian refugees perished.

The actions of the SS *Henry Bacon* had prevented the main convoy from suffering further loss. The Germans, seeing what they thought was an easy target, focused all their efforts on sinking her, only to discover the men on board were prepared to fight back. This tied up their aircraft until they ran low on fuel and had to return to their bases. The heroism of the men who gave up their places on the lifeboats, knowing full well it meant they would not survive, was recognized later, and many medals were awarded posthumously.

CHAPTER EIGHTEEN

An End to Hostilities

Upon our return from RA64, HMS *Savage* undertook Home Fleet duties, before once again we were called upon to undergo a Kola run.

This did not go down well with some of the crew. Rats was one of those who complained, saying it was ridiculous and, with what the Russians had achieved recently, did they really need any more supplies? The Soviets were virtually knocking on Hitler's front door by all accounts, and he wondered if any of the cargoes we were escorting were even getting to the front line.

I offered him a wry smile and told him there was nothing we could do about it. We went where they sent us. However, I did agree with him the war could not go on for very much longer.

He then asked me what I intended to do when it did eventually come to an end.

I thought for a while before I responded. Ever since I was little I had wanted to join the Navy. That was even before the war started. I told him I believed that I might just stay on when it was all over, as I thought there was plenty of the world still to see.

He agreed there certainly was. And there were plenty of warmer places to visit too. All I had seen recently was snow and ice, in between getting shot at. It was not exactly what I had dreamed of when I was younger, when I had looked out from the battlements of Berwick. There had to be more to sailing than I had experienced so far. Peacetime sailing had got to be more enjoyable than this, I thought.

I wondered about what he had said for a while. I definitely wanted to travel more when the war was over, but I did not want to see any more of the Arctic. I thought I had that particular part of the world covered.

HMS *Savage's* role in convoy JW65, along with the destroyer HMS *Scourge*, was to provide close escort for the aircraft carrier HMS *Trumpeter*, the convoy setting sail on 12 March 1945. With the weather easing somewhat, the ships made good progress and we were left alone. That was until we were approaching the mouth of the Kola Inlet, where the 'wolf packs' were known to concentrate, waiting to attack the ships as they funnelled into the estuary on the final leg to Murmansk.

In spite of the escort's best efforts, we were unable to prevent two merchant ships, SS *Horace Bushnell* and SS *Thomas Donaldson*, and the frigate HMS *Lapwing*, from being torpedoed and eventually sunk. As the remainder of the ships made their way through the ice floes towards the port, thoughts turned on how to get the ships safely out of the inlet when embarking on the return convoy.

With our Asdic suffering problems due to the sea conditions, Rear Admiral Cunninghame-Graham, the convoy commander on board HMS *Diadem*, came up with a plan. We would sail at midnight, and instead of the usual two columns, the ships were to form in three, thus making the run out of the inlet that much quicker. The hunting groups would start operations two hours before the main convoy was to set sail, a lot later than normal, in the hope that any U-boat commanders alert to the situation would not expect the main body of the convoy to pass until much later. The ships would also take a slightly different route than normal, but four destroyers would sail the usual route at high speed, all the time dropping depth charges to keep the U-boats at bay. With any luck, by the time the U-boat commanders realized what was going on, the ships would be well out of the danger zone and on their way.

Thus convoy RA65 set sail at midnight on 23 March 1945, Cunninghame-Graham's plan being put into action with total success. By the time the Germans were aware of what had happened, the convoy was clear away, and we suffered no more enemy activity on the journey home.

RA65 was to be the last Arctic convoy I sailed on. There would be two more convoys to Russia, one sailing just before the war's end and the last just after it had finished.

News was now reaching the crew that the end of the war was imminent. Adolf Hitler had committed suicide in his bunker in Berlin on 30 April, and German forces were fighting a last-ditch battle in the rubble of the capital. Russian soldiers were pouring into the city, and British and American forces were advancing into Germany from the west.

But before the war ended, HMS *Savage* was to take part in one last action. Four days before the German unconditional surrender and victory in Europe was declared, the ship took part in our last offensive operation of the war, codenamed Operation Judgement, supporting three aircraft carriers as they conducted air strikes against shipping west of Narvik.

For the crew of HMS *Savage*, the news the war had ended was received with a certain amount of caution. It almost seemed like an anti-climax. The Captain made an announcement over the ship's tannoy system, and that was that. Almost six years of fighting, of which I myself had taken an active part in three, had now come to a sudden end. However, we were all well aware the Nazis were not to be trusted, there still being many U-boats at sea. Had the news reached them, we wondered? Would some of their commanders accept the fact they had been defeated? Nobody knew for certain, and so, despite hostilities officially coming to an end, each ship operated on a heightened state of alert.

For Norway, the end of German occupation came on the same day. On 5 May, German forces in Denmark surrendered, and on the same day a message was sent to the Norwegian Resistance, which was passed on to the German commander in Norway, General Franz Böhme. This message gave instructions on how he was to make contact with Allied General Headquarters. Böhme made a radio broadcast on the evening of 7 May, telling all German forces to adhere to the capitulation plans.

Following this broadcast, the Norwegian Resistance, the Milorg, numbering more than 40,000, were immediately mobilized and asked to occupy public buildings, including police stations and the Royal Palace. Overnight, an interim Norwegian administration was set up.

The following day, 8 May 1945, which became known for evermore as VE Day, an Allied military mission arrived in the Norwegian capital, Oslo, and the conditions of the surrender were laid out. This included the German High Command agreeing to arrest all Nazi Party members, disarm and intern all SS troops and send German regular soldiers to designated areas. Over the next few days 13,000 exiled Norwegian troops and 30,000 British and American soldiers were sent into the country.

Norway had finally been liberated.

Now the Germans had surrendered in Norway and the country was under the temporary control of Allied forces whilst the Norwegian government, who had been living in exile in Great Britain, waited to be repatriated, Olaf, the Crown Prince of Norway, who had also been reluctantly exiled to Britain for the duration of the war, decided to return with his family. Not only was he eager to get back to his homeland, he knew his return would be a huge boost to the morale of the population, who had suffered extreme hardship whilst under the tyranny of Nazi occupation.

HMS *Savage* was chosen as one of the ships to provide the escort for the returning royal family upon their repatriation on 13 May 1945. This came as wonderful news to the crew. The feeling of euphoria at having won the war was still apparent throughout the ship, and to be chosen for such a prestigious duty was the icing on the cake for us. As for me, I felt an affinity to Norway. My voyages to the Arctic had included passing along the country's coastline on many an occasion, and now to be able to sail into Oslo harbour and deliver their royal family back to the Norwegians was a fine way to finish off my wartime experiences.

It was a bright, sunny Sunday when the *Savage* sailed up the 20-mile stretch of Oslo fjord, behind the Norwegian ship HNoMS *Stord*, which was leading the flotilla. The Crown Prince, royal family and returning government sailed aboard the minelayer HMS *Apollo*. The good weather reflected the mood of everyone on board, and from all the flags I could see flying on the houses dotted along the hillsides, the raised spirits of the Norwegian people were clearly evident. As the ship slowly and peacefully made her way in, people could be seen waving and cheering at us, the crew joining in with the celebrations and waving back.

Standing on the foredeck, leaning against the port gunwale, I grinned at Rats. This was a wonderful experience. He told me this would be a day we would remember for the rest of our lives and we should take it all in and enjoy it. After the Kola run, we deserved this time to rejoice in the victory we had won.

I had to agree. We had all gone through so much to achieve this day.

And then something in the water caught my eye. A number of small boats and dinghies had set out to meet us, the occupants of which were calling to us and waving flags. A young girl in a small dinghy wearing a red pyjama suit called up in perfect English:

'Hey . . . can I come aboard?'

I looked to Rats. 'What do you reckon?'

'Not really appropriate . . . but you know what. Bugger what's appropriate. Someone chuck her a line.'

A sailor further along the gunwale quickly grabbed a rope and threw it to her. A couple of minutes later, the girl was on board and, to the surprise of everyone, started kissing every man she could get hold of. Her excitement at being liberated was infectious, and although she should not have been on board a warship, no officer was prepared to enforce protocol, letting the men enjoy themselves and take in the happy atmosphere.

Eventually, the ship docked at the quayside. A gangplank was lowered, and the girl, still smiling and blowing kisses, was let off.

A large crowd had gathered to welcome the Crown Prince home. In amongst the cheering Norwegians I could see British and American servicemen, men who had been sent to take the surrender and ensure the German troops were disarmed and corralled into hastily constructed prison camps and detention centres, ready for processing. There were a number of large cages further along the quayside containing captured Germans, guarded by heavily armed British soldiers.

A day or so later, I was given the job of manning the gangway, and no sooner had I taken up my position on the quayside than I was approached by a British soldier. He was wearing the red beret of the Parachute Regiment. On his arm was the emblem of the 1st Airborne Division. The man looked fit and well but was slightly dishevelled in appearance, unshaven and bleary-eyed. He was carrying a kitbag over his shoulder and was armed to the teeth, carrying various weapons that, looking at his war-weary face, he had probably used many times over the last few months.

He spoke to me in a broad Yorkshire accent asking if there was any chance of a meal. Along with his comrades he had been living off hard tack since they had arrived in Oslo and, due to the Germans having cleared out most of the supplies, had not been able to get decent food anywhere.

Upon hearing his accent I asked him where he was from, and when he told me Leeds, I said I knew it well, having joined up there. I asked him to follow me and led him across the gangplank and on to the ship.

The paratrooper followed me through the walkways, ducking his head as he stepped into the mess deck. Seeing a group of friends sitting at one of the tables, each of them eating a bowl of steaming stew, I headed in their direction.

I explained to them the paratrooper's plight and asked if someone could get him a bowl of stew. One of the lads got up and went to get him some food. The hungry paratrooper sat down, placing his kitbag to the side. A few moments later, the sailor returned, putting a bowl of stew and a cup of kye on the table in front of him.

He was extremely grateful, spooning the warm stew into his mouth and eating it hungrily. He told us again how finding decent food was becoming a bit of a problem. The Norwegians had been left with virtually nothing, and half of them were starving.

He went on to tell us the Parachute Regiment had been called away from operations in Denmark only eight days previously and had launched the mission to Norway after only four days' preparation. It had been a very quick turnaround, he explained. He had been with the advance party that flew out on 9 May, their job to secure the airfields, maintain some law and order and oversee the German surrender. He told us that some of the Germans had looked happy the whole thing was over, but others had been very arrogant, not quite believing or accepting they had lost the war.

In total, a mere 6,000 airborne troops had been sent to disarm and control 350,000 German soldiers. The 1st Airborne Division was employed to assist in the recovery of prisoners of war as well as in allocating German units to staging areas. They also put the Germans to the job of disarming their minefields. The men kept control until the main forces landed a few days later. Their final duty was to conduct the welcoming ceremony for the arrival of Crown Prince Olaf and his family.

Once the soldier had finished his meal he thanked us for our hospitality and, grabbing his kitbag, opened it, put his hand in and pulled out a pistol. It was a German Luger.

'Here you go, pal,' he said, handing it to the sailor sitting next to him. 'A little souvenir for you. Took it off some Nazi officer the other day that my unit's been guarding.'

The sailor took it from him and thanked him. The paratrooper told him it was perfectly safe and there were no bullets in it. The sailor could not believe his luck.

Next, he pulled out a smaller pistol and gave it to the man sitting across the table, who took it gratefully.

Finally he pulled out a larger weapon. I saw immediately it was an MP40 machine pistol, otherwise known as a Schmeisser. He offered it to me, but I shook my head.

'No thanks, mate,' I replied. 'Give it to someone else. I'm just glad you enjoyed the food.'

A grateful matelot took the weapon from him and he rose to leave. I led him from the mess deck and back out to the quayside, where he turned to shake my hand and thanked me once more for my hospitality. It was clear to me that this man had fought hard in this war and that it was down to people like him that we had achieved the final victory. Giving him a bowl of stew had been the least I could do.

I watched as he walked away with his kitbag once again slung over his shoulder, heading back to guard the prisoner cages along the quayside. I wondered if he would be back if he got hungry again, or if the Army would get their act together and set up proper kitchens for their men. I had enjoyed the man's company and wondered if our paths would ever cross again.

The following day, I was granted some shore leave and decided to explore Oslo on my own. I enjoyed the openness of the city and the upbeat nature of its inhabitants, despite the hardships they had endured for the past five years. Everywhere I went, people smiled at me, some of the men shaking my hand and clapping me on the shoulder, whilst the women planted kisses upon my cheeks. I had no idea what they were saying, but it did not matter. I understood by their actions they were very grateful to me for helping to liberate them from the Nazis. However, many of the shops and stores I passed were boarded up. At first I thought it was to protect them from the fighting, but I was to learn later it was due to the Germans having commandeered all the food and anything else of any value for their troops, leaving the civilian population to starve.

After a few hours, feeling thirsty and in need of a beer, I found a small bar in a back street and entered. A small group of Norwegian men stood in the corner, celebrating loudly and laughing. I walked to the bar and ordered a beer. Fortunately the barman spoke English. He apologized, telling me they had no beer and that all he could offer me was a soft drink. My thirst getting the better of me, I accepted an orange juice and went to sit in the opposite corner to the raucous Norwegians.

After a couple of minutes, I was approached by one of them, a tall man of around thirty-five years old, with a beard, wearing a woollen pullover and hat. He held out his hand and asked me to join him and his friends. They were celebrating the liberation and, as I was alone, I was more than welcome to celebrate with them.

Not wanting to appear rude, I accepted his invitation and asked if there was anything stronger to drink other than orange juice. The man tapped his pocket and winked at me, telling me not to worry about that. He introduced himself as Arvid Neilsen, and after I had shaken his hand and been introduced to the rest of the group, I told them my name, that I was from HMS *Savage* and was pleased to meet them all.

I joined Arvid and his friends at their table and no sooner had I sat down than the Norwegian took a flask from his pocket and poured a clear liquid into my glass. I asked what it was and was told it was Akvavit, a local spirit made from potatoes.

The group of Norwegians proved to be very good company, and I spent an enjoyable hour or so with them, taking soft drinks from the bar and then adding the potent Scandinavian spirit to it. The barman looked on but said nothing. He seemed happy enough with what was going on. Soon enough we were all feeling the effects, and the general mood was one of conviviality, friendship and mutual respect.

Arvid told me he had once been in the merchant navy, and when I asked him which ship he had sailed on I was surprised to hear it was the *Cutty Sark*. He asked if I had heard of her, and when I told him I had and that she was probably the most famous clipper in the world, he explained that she was used as a training ship from the early 1920s until just before the war.

After a while, I drained my drink and stood up to go. Arvid put up a hand to stop me. He invited me to go back with him to his home to meet his wife. He wanted her to have the opportunity to pass on her gratitude to me for what I and my countrymen had done for them. He also told me he had another bottle of Akvavit there that we could open. Not wanting to appear ungrateful, I agreed, and so the two of us set off, after first saying goodbye to Arvid's friends.

A few minutes later, Arvid led me to a small, comfortable flat not far from the bar. Upon entering, we were greeted by a small, blonde woman, around five years younger than her husband. At first she looked unsure as to what a British sailor was doing there, but after Arvid had explained, she grabbed me by the shoulders and kissed me on both cheeks. She then proceeded to babble away at me in Norwegian.

I turned to Arvid, bewildered, not understanding a word she was saying, and he laughed as he translated. She was telling me how welcome I was and how grateful and thankful they all were to us for helping to liberate their country from the Nazis. I asked him to tell her how happy I was to be there, and he duly translated.

Arvid then walked into the sitting room, pulled back a rug and lifted a loose floorboard. He pulled out an almost full bottle of what was presumably Akvavit before replacing the floorboard and smoothing back the rug. He took two glasses from a nearby cupboard, and we both sat at the kitchen table.

His wife then began to speak again. She looked a little upset. After she had finished, Arvid translated once more. She was telling me she was sorry for being unable to offer me anything to eat. She apologized for the lack of hospitality. Arvid explained that the Germans had taken everything. They had not had anything substantial to eat for months. Nobody had. He told me they had been especially cruel, right to the end, even when they knew all was lost, and had left them with nothing.

I told them not to worry about feeding me as we had plenty to eat on the ship and I would not go hungry. I accepted the glass of Akvavit Arvid handed to me and sipped at it thoughtfully.

Arvid continued to inform me that the Nazis had commandeered as much food as they could find for themselves and that the Norwegians were now living on whatever they could get their hands on. He feared that until the Red Cross or the British could get the place organized, people might actually starve.

After a few minutes, Arvid stood up and took out an old gramophone from a cupboard. He wound it up and once it was working he took out a record and placed it on the turntable.

Once he lowered the needle, music filled the room. He smiled as he told me that it had been a long while since they had been able to enjoy freedoms such as this and that they needed to make the most of it.

No sooner had the record played out than he put the needle back to the start and played it again. He apologized at the lack of variety, but he only had the one record. The music was not exactly to my taste, and to have it played over and over would normally have got on my nerves. However, the man's character and obvious happiness at being able to act freely now the Germans were gone was infectious, and I found myself smiling and even tapping my feet to the beat.

After a while I asked him what his story was. How had the occupation been for him? Arvid sighed and rubbed his face. His happy demeanour was instantly replaced by a look of great sadness. I instantly regretted asking the question. I had not intended to distress the man. I started to apologize, but he put up his hand, cutting me off and telling me there was no need to. He rubbed his face and then spoke.

It had been hard, he told me, particularly for the women. He had been a member of the Milorg, the Norwegian Resistance, pretty much from the moment the Nazis had arrived. He had been involved in many operations: intelligence-gathering, aiding escaping prisoners, espionage and other things besides. More lately he had been carrying out sabotage missions, hitting the Germans and then heading over the border into Sweden to escape them.

Unfortunately, a few weeks previously, he had been caught by the Gestapo and tortured. He had been convinced they were going to execute him, but then, as it became apparent to the Germans that the war was lost, they put him in a cell and either forgot about him or just left him there to stew. He presumed that, with the war about to end, they did not want to be held accountable for murdering him. When the surrender came, they simply opened the doors and let him go. He had headed straight home and had been there ever since.

I was amazed at his story. There had been much more to this war than my own personal experiences. Millions of people throughout the world had been affected by it, the survivors each having their own individual stories, enduring their own hardships and private hells.

After a couple more drinks, I felt I needed to return to the ship before it got too late. I was feeling hungry by now and did not want the alcohol to go to my head.

After bidding farewell and promising to visit the following day, I set off back to the ship. While I walked I pondered Arvid and his wife's situation. They were good people and did not deserve to be struggling the way they were, particularly as it was no fault of their own. If I could help them in any way, then I felt that I should.

The following day, I returned to their small apartment. I was wearing a Burberry raincoat, the belt pulled tightly around my waist. Once inside, I headed straight for the kitchen and pulled from my coat tins of fruit, corned beef and butter, which I had taken from the mess stock, placing them all on the table.

They were both ecstatic. Arvid shook me by the hand vigorously and his wife kissed me again, tears of joy running down her cheeks. I told her to think nothing of it and that we had plenty of food on the ship. I could not let them go hungry, especially when they had been so kind to me the previous day.

For the next few days, I visited the Neilsens. Each time I brought with me whatever the mess could spare, until the time came when our own mess stocks would have run short if I had continued. However, as the month wore on, food distribution in the city became a little better, and when the time came for HMS *Savage* to leave, I knew my Norwegian friends would be fine.

In early June, HMS *Savage* was ordered to return to Britain and to go to Chatham docks for a refit. As the day got closer for HMS *Savage* to leave Oslo, Arvid asked me for a photograph, which was duly taken and placed upon his mantelpiece.

As we said our goodbyes, I promised to come back to the city and visit them in peacetime, and it was with much sadness that I said my final farewell to them both and the ship set sail back to Britain.

Unfortunately, through no fault of my own, I was never able to keep my promise to the Neilsens and would never see them again. Many years later, I made enquiries with the mayor of Oslo as to their whereabouts but was told they had both sadly passed away.

CHAPTER NINETEEN

Warmer Waters

After her refit, HMS *Savage* was attached to HMS *Excellent*, the gunnery school in Portsmouth, as a firing ship. Now the war had ended, and with the ship stuck down in Portsmouth, I decided my time with the Royal Navy had come to a natural end. Having asked to leave, I was discharged in June of 1946 and then moved back to Hornchurch, where I took up a position in a car factory.

It was only a matter of a few months before the sea again called to me and I once more got the wanderlust. There were still so many places I wanted to visit, so much of the world I wished to see. My time in the Royal Navy had been filled with danger and the icy horrors of the Arctic Ocean. Now I wanted something different. Having spent only a short time, during Operation Torch, in the sunny Mediterranean, I now craved to be on a ship again, but this time away from snow and ice and instead in warmer, more hospitable places.

And so, in the autumn of 1946, I made the journey to the Merchant Navy offices in Tower Hill, London, and hobbled in. I had had an accident involving my foot at work a few weeks previously, and it had still not quite healed.

I approached the desk and informed the recruiting officer of my wishes. He told me he did not see a problem but that I would have to join at a level lower than my final Royal Navy rank, which did not bother me at all. I was also required to take a medical. He advised me to apply at a later date, when my foot was fully healed, but I told him it was now or never; should I leave the offices without signing, then I would be unlikely to return.

I was sent upstairs for the medical and despite the problem with my foot, I passed it successfully and was told to go home and await further instructions.

A few weeks later, I joined the crew of the SS *Winchester Victory*, at Tilbury docks, and immediately set sail for Port Said, Egypt, which was to be the base of operations for the ship in the

Mediterranean and Red Seas. Along with her sister ship, the now famous *Empire Windrush*, the *Winchester Victory* was to be used for transporting troops to places around the region, an undertaking the sailors nicknamed the 'Medlock Run'. As we sailed further south, I could feel the weather warming up and knew I had made the right decision in going back to sea. Being confined in a factory was just not for me. I felt at home on board ship. This was all I had wanted to do as a child, and now there were no U-boats or German dive bombers to worry about I could get on with enjoying sailing, without the fear of a torpedo hitting the sides or a bomb dropping on deck.

The accommodation on the merchant ships was luxury compared to what I had experienced on Royal Navy destroyers. Instead of having to sling a hammock or crash out wherever I could find a space in noisy and cramped conditions, the *Winchester Victory* provided cabins for the crew. Although I had to share with three other men, this was sheer luxury compared to what I had endured on the *Milne* and *Savage*. We were even provided with clean white bed sheets and warm blankets.

I quickly made good friends with one of my cabin mates, a man by the name of Mick with the same adventurous and 'happy-go-lucky' attitude as I had. The two of us made a pact that now the war was over, we would enjoy our trips around the sunspots of the Mediterranean as much as we possibly could. We had worked hard, now it was the time to play hard.

As we sailed through the Straits of Gibraltar and into the wider Mediterranean, I looked out to sea and, in the distance to the port side, I could just make out the large rock that overlooked the British Overseas Territory. I was reminded of the time I had spent there, prior to Operation Torch, almost five years ago, and for a moment I smiled. That particular run ashore had been a lot of fun. But at the same time I also felt a deep sadness, as the memory of the sinking of HMS *Martin* also entered my thoughts. I counted my blessings. I was able to be here during peacetime, to enjoy the place, something many of my fellow seamen from back then would never be able to do.

On arrival in Port Said it became clear we would be holed up there for some time. We were to embark troops for transport to the port of Massawa in Eritrea, from where they would head for Asmara, the capital, which had been part of the Italian Empire until the British had kicked them out after the Battle of Keren in 1941. Eritrea was now being administered by the British until the government could make a decision on the African nation's future.

With little to do, and it being too hot to work for long, permission was given for the men to go ashore. Mick and I jumped at the chance, taking a launch to the jetty, to visit the bars and markets of the city

On one such day, we decided to go for a walk around the perimeter of the city and take in the sights, as a change to our normal routine. Wherever we walked, the streets were filled with people of all colours, wearing flowing garments, colourful headdresses and scarves to keep off the hot sun's rays. Most of the women wore veils over their faces, as was the custom with their religion. All around, the air was filled with the noise and bustle of a busy city, the two of us having to quickly move out of people's way as they hurried past. Street chefs cooked and sold curious looking dishes that gave off wonderful aromas of herbs and spices, fragrances I had never experienced before. We passed magnificent looking domed buildings, the legacy of Port Said's Ottoman past, large white structures coloured with gold, their minarets pointing to the sky in an almost imperious manner.

After a while Mick tugged at my arm and pointed to my right. He asked what I thought was going on. I looked in the direction he was indicating and saw a tall building to our left. It had large double doors, made from what looked like the finest oak, which were wide open. Through the open doorway, we could see a large group of men in lines, bowing down on mats. They were over a hundred in number, and a strange noise was coming from them.

'Looks like they're praying,' I told him.

'Come on,' said Mick. 'Let's go and have a look.'

Our curiosity now fully aroused, we walked to the entrance of the mosque and peered inside. Facing away from us, the men, all on their knees bowing forward, occasionally rose to chant together, before bowing down once more. At the far end of the room an imam read from the Koran. I could not understand a word of what was being said but was nevertheless fascinated by the spectacle.

Mick stepped past me into the room to get a better view.

Almost immediately someone in the street yelled in our direction. I turned my head to see a small group of men shouting and screaming. At first I did not realize on whom they were venting their ire, but it soon became apparent it was the two of us.

Mick could not understand what was upsetting them so much, and when I told him we might have offended them, his confusion was not diminished, as we had done nothing other than observe. I remarked that maybe we should not actually be there and perhaps this was the reason.

By now some of the men who had been praying were looking over to us, having been disturbed from their prayers. They began to stand, not looking one bit pleased.

'I think we'd better get out of here,' I suggested. 'And I think we'd better be quick about it too.'

Mick stepped back into the street and agreed it was probably the best course of action. The disturbance had attracted the attention of more people, and an angry mob was starting to form. Someone picked up a rock and threw it at us, narrowly missing my head.

'Run!' I yelled.

Mick did not need any persuading, and a few seconds later we were sprinting through the streets, hotly followed by an incensed crowd that was gathering in numbers as we fled. We dodged between the people we had seen only minutes earlier, past the wonderful looking buildings and the street vendors, no longer interested in the sights or smells of what Port Said had to offer. We had only one thing on our minds and that was to get back to the ship as quickly as we could.

Without looking behind, I ran as fast as I could, grateful I had kept myself fit since leaving the Royal Navy. I was aware of Mick keeping up with me and also of one or two rocks bouncing off walls to our side as the crowd threw them at us two fleeing British sailors.

Eventually, we reached the dockside and could see the ship's boat tied to the jetty. On board were a few other lads from the *Winchester Victory*. They looked relaxed after having enjoyed a few hours ashore, completely oblivious to the predicament of the two shipmates who were now bearing down on them at full speed, pursued by a baying crowd of irate Egyptians.

'Quick!' I shouted to the coxswain, who looked at me in bewilderment. 'Get us back to the ship before they kill us.'

Then, seeing the advancing crowd behind us, the coxswain stepped on to the jetty and untied the boat. As he jumped back aboard, Mick and I threw ourselves into the boat beside him.

One of our colleagues, taken by surprise at this odd turn of events, shouted to us, asking what on earth was going on and what had we done to upset them. He threw the cigarette he had been smoking over the side and ducked as a rock bounced off the side of the boat, splashing into the sea beside him.

'Jesus!' he exclaimed. 'Get us out of here.'

Quickly the coxswain gunned the outboard motor and the boat headed away from the jetty, the shouts of the crowd mixing with the engine noise as more rocks splashed into the sea around us. A few better aimed shots hit a couple of seamen on board, and they cursed loudly, both at those on the shore throwing them, and at the pair of us who had caused the problem.

The coxswain yelled at us, calling us idiots and asking why the locals were so mad at us.

'I only popped my head into one of their mosques to see what it was all about,' explained Mick. 'I don't know why they kicked off like that.'

'It's a bloody good job they didn't catch you,' said one of the crew, ducking, as another stone whizzed by. 'They'd have probably ripped you limb from limb.'

He told us that non-believers going inside a mosque uninvited during prayers was 'a big no-no'. It was very disrespectful, he said.

Eventually, we arrived at the ship and, once on board, finally got our breath back. We decided that it was probably best not to bother going ashore for a few days, to hopefully let matters cool down.

Our escapade ashore had not gone down too well with our colleagues, many of whom also chose to stay on board until the dust settled; and we had to endure some sarcastic remarks from a few of them. But having spent so many years on the Kola run, I had developed a very thick skin, and it did not bother me in the slightest.

* * *

A few days later, with all troops now embarked, the *Winchester Victory* set sail. After the incident with the mosque, I was not sad to see the back of the Egyptian port for a while.

We headed south from Port Said, through the Isthmus of Suez and into the Suez Canal. From the deck, I could see the small towns and villages dotted along its sides and wondered at the feat of engineering it had taken to construct it, almost a hundred years previously. Men astride camels sauntered almost lethargically across the horizon, shimmering in the heat of the afternoon sun. Soon we entered the Great Bitter Lake, a wide open salt water lake that had been dry before the canal's construction. This area was used for ships to pass or to turn around as necessary. The final stretch of the canal took us past the town of Suez itself and out into the vast Red Sea, which would eventually lead to the Indian Ocean should we continue heading that way.

The ship continued south, with Egypt, then Sudan, on our starboard side and Saudi Arabia to port. Looking out to the port side, where I knew the holy city of Mecca to be, far from my vision, I was reminded of Lawrence of Arabia, knowing this was the area in which he famously led the Arab Revolt during the Great War.

Eventually, we arrived at Massawa on the Eritrean coast. From what we could make out it was not in the same league as Port Said, or any of the other ports I had visited before. The harbour area appeared worn and dirty, and what we could see of the town itself looked no better. The ship was slowed to a halt and tied to a grubby, dilapidated jetty. Not long after, the troops were disembarked and they set off towards the hills and their destination of Asmara.

Standing with me at the gunwale as we watched the soldiers making their way off the ship, Mick observed that the place looked a bit of a dump. I had to agree with him. From what we could see, it was hardly Gibraltar. And it was so very hot too.

The heat was, at times, oppressive. It was the polar opposite of the conditions I had experienced on the Arctic convoys. As cold as it had been in the Barents Sea, the heat of the Red Sea was its equal in the discomfort it created. The temperature, at midday, reached an incomprehensible 110° Fahrenheit.

It became impossible to stay below deck for too long, the compartments heating up like ovens. Even on deck, the steel and iron of the superstructure was too hot to touch. Going ashore, despite the apparent lack of anything exciting to do, was probably the best course of action. At least there we might find some shade and maybe a cold drink. Since it was too hot to work, the crew were granted shore leave, and so, along with the rest of the crew, Mick and I went ashore to find a place to cool down and get some refreshment.

Once on dry land, my friend and I set off walking towards a group of trees we had seen from the ship, leaving the rest of the crew in the small town to search for a drink or to find other places to relax. As we walked along the dusty lane we came to a corner that led to an avenue of trees. We decided to follow it. After a couple of minutes we heard something that seemed somewhat out of place in this African backwater. It was music. And not just any music. It was distinctly western and surprisingly modern.

Mick suggested we find out where it was coming from and set off in search of its source. I followed my friend. As we got further along the avenue the music became louder. We then came to a long high wall with an iron entrance gate, and when we looked through the bars, we saw a large swimming pool. At the side of the pool an orchestra was playing and opposite, a sight for our very sore eyes, was a bar with an open area for dancing. In the pool was a mixed group of male and female swimmers, laughing and frolicking. Some bathers sat at tables to the side, drinking beer and smoking.

We opened the gate and entered the premises. As we approached the pool some of those inside who had noticed us come in looked at us curiously. From what I could understand, the group consisted mainly of Italians, or people of Italian descent, the men tanned and handsome, the women dark-haired and very pretty.

'Hey,' said Mick to one of the men who was staring at us. 'What's going on here?'

The man replied in perfect English, but with a strong Italian accent that they were having a party and suggested we get our swimming things and join them. The water, he said, was quite lovely.

I looked at my friend and raised my eyebrows. 'What do you think?'

'What do I think?' he replied. 'I think we should get our swimming things and join them!'

Turning to the young man in the pool, I told him we would not be long.

Without wasting a moment, we rushed back to the ship to get towels and trunks and a few minutes later we had changed and were in the pool with the Italians. To find such an oasis in the middle of what was at first glance, the worst place imaginable to spend any downtime, was the best bit of luck we could have wished for. The memory of being chased through the streets of Port Said by an angry mob had, for the moment, vanished completely.

We spent the whole of the day there, swimming, talking to the Italians and drinking the cold beer that was on offer. We even managed a dance with some of the girls. It was well after two in the morning before we finally bade our farewells and returned to the ship.

Upon our return, one of our cabin mates asked us where we had been all day. When we told him we had been drinking, dancing and swimming in a pool with a group of gorgeous Italian girls and had had a great time, he did not believe us. He told us to 'pull the other one'. He said the place was a total dump and the rest of the crew had been bored out of their heads all day. He accused us both of having sunstroke and told us to stop making stories up.

Mick told him to come along the following day and we would prove to him we were not lying. However, we were not to get the chance to enjoy another day like that. Our cabin mate advised us that had we been on the ship we would have found out we were bound for Port Said the following morning. Whereas he could not wait to get out of the place quickly enough, Mick and I would have liked another day or two in port.

As Mick and I dozed easily, after consuming so much alcohol and expending energy all day, we were woken occasionally by the moaning of our two cabin mates as they tossed and turned in the interminable heat.

I closed my eyes. I had had the best of days, there was no doubt about it. As I drifted off to sleep I realized I was smiling.

CHAPTER TWENTY

An International Incident

Upon arrival at Port Said, the next assignment the *Winchester Victory* was given was to transport troops from Egypt to Toulon in southern France, from where we would then make our way home to Britain.

Well, that was the plan.

It was just south of Malta when the ship developed difficulties with her boiler tubes. The *Winchester Victory* was a mass produced 'Liberty' ship, and this was a common problem in a lot of them. Unable to continue, the ship limped into the Grand Harbour at Valletta, Malta, where she was tied up, her stern to the harbour steps. The weary troops were offloaded to await further transportation, but as for the crew, we were stuck there until the repairs could be carried out.

We arrived in Valletta on a wonderfully sunny day, the harbour full of shipping and colourful *dghajsas* (or *dysos*), small gondola-style boats used as water taxis. From the deck of the *Winchester Victory* the medieval forts of St Elmo and Manoel could clearly be seen, their limestone walls still showing damage from the recent bombing.

Upon hearing from the engineering officer that the spare parts had to be sent from America, and it could take a long time for them to arrive, it was probable we would be holed up in Malta for the next few months. There was nothing to be done other than make the most of it.

Malta had sustained massive bomb damage during the recent siege, and building and repair work was still ongoing wherever we went. The island had been one of the most intensely bombed areas in the whole war, the Germans knowing of its strategic importance for control of the Mediterranean. Had the island capitulated, then the invasion of Sicily and Italy and the victory in North Africa would not have been possible. It was therefore revered by the Allies, so much so that after the war the island was given the George Cross by King George VI, an award to the inhabitants as a whole for their endurance and bravery in the face of a very violent enemy.

The island was also very hospitable to British armed forces and those who had served in the services during the war, and so, when my friends and I visited the bars of Valletta, we were always made to feel very welcome.

As we were to be stuck here for some considerable time, Mick and I became regulars at various bars in the town. One in particular, the 'Morning Star', became a frequent haunt of ours, and we would often find ourselves staggering back to the ship in the evening after a particularly heavy session on the beer and spirits.

One morning, Mick and I were given the task of painting the ship's hull, more to keep us occupied than anything else, and so a couple of bosun's chairs were slung over the stern for us to work from. Out of sight of the deck, we were able to go through the motions of painting, all the time chatting up the locals as they walked by. However, this was not to last, and soon the ship was moved across the harbour to the military docks to await the spare parts coming from America.

A large, fancy looking yacht was docked not far from the *Winchester Victory*, and someone told us it was the royal yacht of King Farouk of Egypt. At ten o'clock the following morning an awful noise came from the direction of the royal vessel, and the crew of the *Winchester Victory* stood on deck looking out to see what it could be.

A band had been set up on the deck and they were practising. The noise they were creating was excruciating to our ears. It sounded like a very bad rendition of La Paloma, but it was such a poor attempt we could very easily have been mistaken.

Many of the sailors grimaced as the band rehearsed. There was no way we could put up with that din all day long. It was not so much that it sounded like they were strangling a cat, it was as though they were murdering hundreds of them! The screeching of the instruments went on for a long while, the notes flat and out of tune. Working on deck became a pain to the ears, and it was not long before some of the crew got totally fed up. The Captain had shrugged his shoulders and told us there was nothing he could do about it. It was not his ship, and it was up to her own captain to shut them up.

Even after a couple of days the din coming from the royal yacht had not improved; in no way could it ever be called music. And so, with no other option, the crew decided to take matters into our own hands.

The very next day, bang on time at 10.00 am, the awful orchestra of King Farouk's royal yacht set up to practise. No sooner had they started their awful cacophony than the men of the *Winchester Victory* put our plan into motion. Each of us, armed with spanners, hammers, kitchen utensils and any other metal tool we could lay our hands on, formed our own merry band. Together we banged them against the bulkhead, creating a loud, unpleasant, clanging din that drowned out the caterwauling from across the water.

Almost immediately the band stopped playing, unable to hear themselves, and looked across at the *Winchester Victory*. We raised our 'instruments' in greeting. As the band on the royal yacht struck up again, the crew once more hit the bulkhead with our tools, forcing them to stop playing once more.

This went on for a number of minutes, before the band finally gave up, gathered up their instruments and took them away below decks. A large cheer went up from the *Winchester Victory* as they disappeared out of sight.

The following day, the same thing happened again. As soon as the band started playing, the crew drowned them out with our own orchestra of pots, pans, spanners and hammers.

However, the Captain was beginning to get nervous about the whole thing.

'You're in danger of causing an international incident,' he warned us. 'This has to stop. I know they're not exactly the Royal Philharmonic, but you'll just have to put up with it. Anyway, as soon as the new boiler tubes arrive, we'll be on our way.'

When the Captain returned to the bridge, Mick commented that he had been enjoying himself. He thought the whole thing was very funny. However, we all agreed that it had been quite rude of us, but something had had to be done to protect our ears.

That evening, we decided to take the launch across the Grand Harbour for a night out in Valletta. The return launch left at midnight so we had to ensure we gave it plenty of time to get back to the harbour steps.

We spent the evening visiting our favourite bars, most of our time being spent in the Morning Star, where we enjoyed live music from a very talented accordion player, danced with local girls and drank as much beer and spirits as we could manage. We had such a good time that when I looked at my watch after ordering another round of drinks, I was shocked to see how late it had got.

I called to Mick, who was sitting at a table talking to a pretty young lady. I told him we had to get a move on as it had already gone midnight. Leaving our unfinished drinks, the two of us raced through the steep narrow streets back to the harbour steps. By the time we arrived it was half past midnight and we knew it was too late. The boat back to the *Winchester Victory* had long since left, and the water taxis had stopped working at eleven.

'We can't even get a *dyso*,' I said, frowning. 'Looks like we're stuck here.'

'Maybe,' replied Mick. 'I don't fancy staying here until morning, though. I need my bed.'

Suddenly there was a noise to our right and out of the darkness a smart white launch approached, a well-dressed officer standing on its deck.

I called out to him. 'Hey! Is there any chance you can give us a lift back to our ship?'

Replying in a strong accent, the officer enquired which ship we belonged to.

'Er, the *Winchester Victory*,' I called back.

The officer laughed. 'Then in that case . . . absolutely not. You are from the ship that has insulted our king. So no, we will not give you a lift.'

And with that the launch carried on past us. We looked to each other and frowned. It seemed that, as we probably suspected, our little orchestra on board the *Winchester Victory* had not gone down too well with those on the Egyptian royal yacht. Can't take a joke, some people, I thought.

And then Mick called out after them. 'We're not bothered . . . we'll swim.'

I looked at him in consternation. What on earth was he talking about? He had clearly had too much to drink if he thought we could swim across the Grand Harbour.

Without another word or any kind of warning, Mick stepped forward and dived into the water. When he surfaced he kicked out and began to swim in the direction of the ship. Not wanting to be left alone on the harbour steps, I decided to follow and also stepped forward and dived in, following my friend.

Fortunately, halfway across, there was a buoy where we were able to catch our breath ready for the next part of the swim. I cursed myself for having followed my friend into the water. After going through so much during the past few years, if I got cramp and drowned here, it would be a most ridiculous way to die. Although I had drunk more than my fill, I had quickly sobered up, my concentration fully on the task ahead.

After getting my breath back and cursing my friend's foolhardiness, I kicked off again to the next buoy, until eventually we made it to the quayside and were able to get back on board the ship. We both changed out of our wet clothes and made our way to our bunks. The two men we shared the cabin with appeared to be asleep. However, one turned and spoke to us.

'What happened to you two? How did you get back?'

'We swam across the harbour,' I said, matter-of-factly.

'Don't be ridiculous,' came the reply. The man turned his back on me and closed his eyes again.

I smiled to myself. Yes, I thought, it was ridiculous. But at the same time, it was also very much true. How many people could claim to have swam across the Grand Harbour in Malta? And to have done so in the middle of the night after consuming a skinful of beer. Not many, I thought, not many.

And yes, my cabin mate was quite correct.

It was totally ridiculous!

CHAPTER TWENTY-ONE

Piraeus and Naples

With the delivery of new boiler tubes from America, it was not long before the *Winchester Victory* was back on the move, heading back to our home base at Port Said. I hoped the inhabitants had now calmed down after our faux pas at the mosque a few months earlier.

Upon arrival at the port a few days later, we immediately took on board more soldiers for another Medlock run. This time they were headed to Haifa, Israel, where we were to pick up more troops for onward transportation to Piraeus, the port town near Athens.

As the ship sailed into Piraeus a few days later, a number of smaller craft were also in the water. Fancying another run ashore but having no Greek money to spend, Mick and I opened the portholes of our cabin and called to a passing bumboat. After a few minutes of hard bartering, we had enough money for a night out, but were now minus our bed sheets, an exchange both of us thought was worth it.

For me, this life was proving to be all I had wanted it to be. The horrors of the Barents Sea were fast becoming just a bad memory, and quitting my job on Civvy Street to join the merchant navy was the best decision I had ever made. I had worked hard for years on the destroyers, enduring terrible hardships and, although I still pulled my weight on the *Winchester Victory*, I now had more opportunity for some fun and was determined to make the most of it. After all, I had served my time and thoroughly deserved it. To make it even better, this was all being done in the heat of the Mediterranean and not in the frozen wastes of the Arctic Ocean.

Once all our duties had been carried out, we set off into the town to check out the drinking establishments and see what Piraeus had to offer. Unaware of the political situation in Greece at the time, the two of us naively sauntered into town expecting to find plenty of bars full of life, much as we had done at the other ports we had visited. The truth of the matter was, at the time Greece was in the middle of a civil war. Government forces, supported by Britain and America had been fighting an uprising by the communist-backed EAM, a resistance group that had refused to hand in their weapons at the end of the war. Since the Greek king was restored to the throne in 1946 the EAM had been conducting a full-scale guerrilla war against government forces.

Wandering into town, and totally ignorant of what was going on around us, we soon found ourselves walking along a quiet, deserted street, late in the afternoon. The shutters on the windows of all the buildings were closed and nobody was sitting at any of the pavement cafés we passed, all their tables being empty.

With the recently acquired drachmas burning a hole in our pockets, we searched unsuccessfully for somewhere open where we could sample the Greek beer. The place looked dead, and Mick was getting frustrated at not being able to find anywhere open to get a drink. He thought the Greeks looked like a boring lot. I had to agree with him and said we would have been better staying on the ship.

And then something at the top of the street caught our eye, causing us to stop walking.

A hundred yards ahead of us, a group of serious looking men had appeared. Disconcertingly, each one of them was armed with a weapon of some kind: rifles, pistols and one or two with what looked like machine guns.

I did not like the look of this one bit. What had we walked into?

And then one of the men raised his weapon and opened fire. Immediately he was joined by other members of the group. The pair of us dived to the ground, bullets whistling above our heads. Some of the men began to shout, and as we raised our heads to look at them we saw they too were now diving for cover.

And then from behind us, more gunfire rang out.

'They're not shooting at *us*,' said Mick, scrambling towards the building at the side of the road.

I glanced behind and saw that my friend was quite right. Further along the street another group of men, also well armed, had started to return fire at the first group. We had inadvertently found ourselves in the middle of a gun battle.

As quickly as I could, I crawled to the side of the road and then stood up, joining Mick who was taking shelter in a doorway.

'We need to get out of here, sharpish,' I said. 'We don't want to get caught in the crossfire.'

There was nowhere for us to escape to, and we realized we would have to wait it out where we stood. To move on or attempt to get out of the way could have been fatal, as either side could easily have mistaken us for members of the group they were fighting, or we might be struck by a stray bullet or ricochet.

After a few more minutes the firing stopped, and it appeared both groups had moved on. Cautiously we looked up and down the street and when we were content it was clear, we both breathed a huge sigh of relief. It was then we realized the doorway in which we had managed to take cover belonged to a café bar, and so we decided to knock on the door.

It was opened by a young woman, and when we entered we saw there were a few customers inside. Using the drachmas we had acquired by selling our bed sheets through the porthole, we spent the rest of the day being introduced to ouzo, the national drink of Greece. It was much later when we returned to the ship.

The following day, the ship was again on the move, taking more troops to Toulon. However, as we sailed through the Straits of Messina, a familiar problem was once again to hit the *Winchester Victory*. Just as before, the boiler tubes developed a defect, and the ship was forced to head again for the nearest port. Limping in at a mere 3–4 knots, we managed to make it to Naples before the tubes finally gave out altogether. It was likely we were now in for another extended stay in a foreign port.

For myself, this was a welcome problem. I had always wanted to visit the country of my mother's birth and although this was an unscheduled stop, I was pleased it would mean I could spend some time in Italy. Pozzuoli, the town where my mother was raised, was a mere 15 miles from the centre of Naples.

However, first impressions were not exactly awe-inspiring. After tying up away from the main entrance to the docks, I was eager to get ashore. Was the country as beautiful as I had imagined? Ever since I was a young boy in Berwick-upon-Tweed, I had always wanted one day to visit Italy and see for myself the country where my mother had spent her formative years. In my mind Italy was a wonderful place, full of beauty, history and wonder. Would it live up to my expectations?

As I and a few shipmates walked through the dock gates shortly after being released from our duties, I was saddened to discover that if the rest of the country was anything like Naples, then I was not going to be impressed one bit. The dock gates opened into the local fish market, and the stench coming from the stalls was overpowering. The heat of the day enhanced the pungent odour to a degree at which we had to cover our noses as we walked by. The stall holders and tradesmen seemed oblivious to it, but for the men disembarking the ship it was almost unbearable.

As we passed a group of men lifting baskets of fish on to a trestle table, their white aprons stained with fish guts and scales, I remarked that this place was a bit of a let down. Mick agreed, commenting that the whole place stank to high heaven. He was not wrong, it was awful.

We soon found out the dock entrance we had used was not the only way out of the port area, the main exit leading directly to the town centre. Once there, we were approached by a group of young boys, gabbling to us in Italian and holding out dog-eared black and white photographs of young women.

'What are they saying?' asked Mick, as a youngster pulled at his arm.

'No idea,' I responded, myself attempting to fend off another young boy.

I watched on as my friend sat down on a low wall and took hold of the photograph the boy was thrusting at him.

'Seester,' said the boy in heavily accented English. 'You like?'

Mick looked at the photograph and then handed it back. 'What on earth are you talking about?'

As his attention was focused on the boy with the photograph, he was unaware that one of the youngster's accomplices was behind him, his hand in the sailor's jacket pocket, fishing for anything of value. I quickly shouted a warning to Mick and he jumped up, grabbing hold of his jacket. Before we had a chance to accost the two thieves, they had turned around and were now sprinting into the crowded town square.

Mick was livid, his face red with rage. He checked his pockets and found they had been unsuccessful in robbing him. It looked like my shout had come just in time. This was a warning to us, and we knew we would have to be more alert to pickpockets in future.

From then on, whenever we would see any of these 'Fagin's boys' as we decided to call them, we would either brush them off or avoid them completely. We also alerted any new sailors we came across to do the same.

We entered the main square. An impressive looking building took up the whole of one side which, we were informed by a passing soldier, was the Royal Palace. However, far from being exclusively reserved for royalty, the building had been taken over by the Navy, Army and Air Force Institute, (NAAFI), for the use of Allied armed forces who were still occupying Italy following the war.

As we entered the building we were further surprised to see a British pub, 'The George and Dragon', had been created for use by British troops. Just outside of this was a wide sweeping staircase that led upstairs to even more areas for recreational activity. A cinema, ballroom and three restaurants were situated along a 20ft wide corridor where a band played and an artist sat at an easel offering sketch portraits for the price of two cigarettes.

We both knew instantly we were going to like it here. Being holed up in Naples for a few months was not going to be such a bad thing.

By far the most popular café bar was the one staffed by a group of NAAFI girls who all wore the uniform of the British Army. As such, they came under military discipline. The girls were billeted on the top floor of the palace and this was strictly out of bounds for any male friends they had. The crew of the *Winchester Victory* enjoyed this bar the most, where we were able to exchange banter with the NAAFI girls, one of whom, much to my pleasure, came from Leeds.

We sat ourselves at a table and I ordered two glasses of beer. When the drinks were delivered I handed over my lira note. After a few minutes, the girl had not returned with my change. As she passed by I asked her if she had it.

She smiled at me. 'Don't worry about it,' she responded in her Yorkshire accent that seemed very out of place in southern Italy. 'We don't have change for lira notes.'

And that was that. Whether she was joking or not, I did not receive any coins, and every subsequent time I paid for anything in the NAAFI bar in this way, they never gave me change for paper money.

One of the advantages of being in the merchant navy was that we were always dressed in civilian clothes, or 'civvies', and so were able to blag our way into the officers' bars and restaurants whenever we fancied it (unless we were asked for our identity cards which would show us to be Able Seamen and not of officer rank). On a few occasions we pretended to be third and fourth officers of a ship and were allowed in to partake in what the officers had at their disposal. However, we preferred the company of the 'other ranks' and the girls in the less pretentious bars, and so spent most of our evenings in them.

It was not long before my charms had an effect on one of the NAAFI workers, a young woman by the name of Joyce Hainsworth. After a somewhat whirlwind romance, we decided to make our relationship permanent and celebrated our engagement at one of the restaurants with ten of my shipmates and a group of Joyce's friends.

However, just like my relationship with Tish, our love affair appeared to be short-lived. One evening when I met up with her, I found her crying. When I asked what the matter was, she informed me the Army were posting her to Graz in Austria and that she was to leave very soon.

I was flabbergasted. Apparently Joyce's superiors had heard about her engagement to a merchant seaman and had instantly organized to move her away from Naples. The pettiness of the whole thing was shocking. Why they would do such a thing was beyond me. The worst feature was we could not do a single thing to stop it. Once the Army's mind was made up, then that was it. We just had to get used to it.

I had known that at any time the new boiler tubes could turn up and the *Winchester Victory* would again be on its way. We had both been aware of this and would have dealt with it when it happened. But to be forced apart by small-minded bureaucrats in such a way was both upsetting and irritating.

With a promise to keep in touch, a tearful Joyce left a few days later.

After Joyce's enforced parting I was feeling down and I needed to be cheered up. As luck would have it, the *Winchester Victory*'s sister ship, the SS *Empire Windrush*, was due to dock in Naples in the next few days, and a message was sent challenging the crew of the *Winchester Victory* to a football match if a suitable pitch could be found. This was just what I needed to boost my spirits.

The challenge duly accepted, the ship's Captain asked the Military Police if they could find a pitch for the match, and once one was found, the two teams set off to play the game, both sides kitted out in football gear.

However, upon arriving at the pitch, we found it occupied by nearly two hundred children and youths, all milling about and encroaching on the playing surface. The pitch itself was not exactly Wembley Stadium, the grass long in some places and dry, dusty brown patches in others. The goalposts, slightly crooked and lop-sided, had no nets and looked in danger of falling down.

As we approached the pitch some of the children saw the ball and tried to knock it out of the hands of the sailor who was carrying it, but he hung on to it protectively. They clearly wanted a kick-about themselves and knew nothing about the match about to go ahead. We stepped out on to the pitch and were immediately surrounded by a large group of youngsters. This was going to be ridiculous. Maybe the match would have to be abandoned before it got started.

However, our worries were short-lived, as one of my teammates found a youngster who spoke English and we quickly explained what was to take place. Once this was transmitted to the other youths still on the pitch, it was soon cleared and the match was able to get underway.

As the game progressed, the crowd of youngsters, who had stayed to watch with interest and had each picked a side to support, became more and more aggressive. As I was in possession of the ball, an opponent clattered into me, knocking me from my feet to lie in the dust. I got up to witness the offending player being pelted with stones by some of the crowd. I held up my hand and they stopped.

'This is mad,' said the player who had tackled me. 'It's supposed to be a friendly game.'

'Yeah,' I said, in response. 'Think on about that the next time you come in at me so hard.'

What the opposition player had said was true. The situation was quite odd. We had not expected the game to generate such interest or for the crowd to be this enthusiastic, and so it was with much relief on both sides when the game finished at two goals each.

It was a few days later when my spell in Naples came to an end. The boiler tubes had arrived, the repair was effected and the ship was once again on her way. As I stood at the stern watching the port disappear from view I realized it was with a huge degree of sadness that I left Italy. Although the first impressions on arrival many weeks previously had been bad, I had quickly grown to love the place. My shipmates and I had had a lot of fun, and the memories of the place would remain with me forever. With a huge sigh, I took one last look, raised my hand in farewell and then went below decks to carry out my duties.

CHAPTER TWENTY-TWO

Farewell to the Sea

In early 1948 I was transferred off the *Winchester Victory*, and while I was waiting for a new ship I went to visit my sister Annette, in London.

It was a Monday morning when I received a telegram asking me to join the Liberty ship SS *Samkey*, which was bound for Cuba with a cargo of ballast taken from the Thames. She was due to set sail from London on 24 January. With the happy thought of a journey to the sunny Caribbean still in my head, I then received another telegram two days later informing me there was a change of plan and I had been reassigned to the RMS *Rangitata*, an ocean liner operated by the New Zealand Shipping Company.

Unbeknown to me at the time, whoever it was at the Merchant Navy office who had made the decision to change my posting had inadvertently saved my life.

The SS *Samkey* set sail from London on time. However, the last contact made with the ship was when she was sailing close to the Azores, heading into the Sargasso Sea. She did not arrive in Cuba, vanishing from the face of the earth within the notorious 'Bermuda Triangle'. She was carrying a crew of forty-three, all of whom are presumed to have perished. A Naval Board of Inquiry held later came to the conclusion she had sunk after the ballast had shifted. There seemed no other explanation, as the weather at the time was known to be fair with no rough seas. The ship was only five years old and had just completed checks in dry dock, all of which she passed. The Board of Inquiry declared the *Samkey* 'was sound in hull design and construction, and was equipped with machinery which was also sound in design and entirely adequate to its task. Further, the vessel was thoroughly well maintained as to both hull and machinery and carried British Corporation Classification.' Furthermore, the ship had four steel life boats that had the capacity to carry three times the number of her crew. The lifeboats could be launched very quickly and each of them carried radios and life-saving equipment. The ship must have sunk very quickly, as no 'Mayday' was transmitted.

The disappearance of the SS *Samkey* remains a mystery to this day.

* * *

I spent the rest of my time in the merchant navy on New Zealand ships, before leaving the service on 23 May 1949. I married Joyce, the NAAFI girl I met at the Royal Palace in Naples, and together we had a son. At first, being an ex-seaman and having joined up at eighteen, finding suitable employment proved difficult. I changed jobs frequently to gain experience. First I worked in the Railway Goods Department as a clerk, but later left to join the local engineers as a rope splicer. Again I switched jobs to become an oxyacetylene operator, cutting out diesel locomotive side plates, which I found to be heavy work. Eventually, the experience I had gained meant I could do a skilled job and so I secured a position in the artificial limb industry, working for Roehampton Hospital's engineering division based in Leeds.

My working section of four different machines was adjacent to another section of three gear cutting machines, which were operated by two men. One of the men, Eddie, was around the same age as I was, the other was much older. Having both served in the armed forces during the war and having a mutual love of horse racing, it was not long before Eddie and I became good friends. We would often spend the working day chatting to each other and also attended social events and made visits to the pub together after work.

And then one day, whilst at work, after being friends for a good many years, a chance remark I made led to a very strange conversation.

'I heard a really good programme on the radio last night,' I said. 'It was about a park in Oslo. It's quite famous for its sculptures and statues. It was really interesting.'

'Oh, I'm sorry I missed it,' replied Eddie. 'I was in Oslo during the war, you know. Well, not really during the war, more at the very end. We were sent over there just after VE Day.'

'Me too,' I replied. 'I was on a destroyer, HMS *Savage*. We escorted the royal family back to Norway.'

Eddie stopped what he was doing, the memories coming back to him.

'You know, when we got there, there was no food around at all. The Germans had requisitioned it from the civilians. Some of them were starving. We had to guard some PoWs and at first, we had to live off hard tack and minimum rations. It wasn't good.'

The talk of Oslo and those times triggered memories within me too. I thought of the two friends I had made, the Neilsens, and wondered how they were doing now.

'You know,' went on my friend. 'The troops were so underfed I even had to go to a ship and scrounge some food. I was really hungry. They were great, the Navy lads. Took me inside and gave me some stew.'

I immediately stopped what I was doing.

'I don't believe it,' I said. 'You didn't happen to give out a load of guns and stuff to the sailors, did you?'

'I did,' said Eddie, frowning. 'But how would you know that?'

I laughed. 'Because I was the matelot who took you on board and got you fed!'

Epilogue

Unfortunately, my marriage to Joyce broke down and we were divorced. In 1978 I married my second wife, Betty, and together we spent many happy years holidaying at our time-share apartment in Puerto de la Cruz in Tenerife, until we gave it up in 2007. We are still very much happily married, living in Yorkshire. I have two grandchildren and three great-grandchildren.

For many years I was a member of various associations: the HMS *Ganges* Association, the North Russia Club and the Russian Convoy Club, attending many reunions throughout the country, until the passage of time caused numbers to dwindle, and the groups were eventually disbanded.

I am the recipient of many campaign medals and was awarded my latest, the seventy-five year anniversary medal, from Russia, as recently as VE Day, 8 May 2020.

* * *

Having reached the age of ninety-seven, I can now look back on all my travels around the world, from Spitzbergen in Norway to Auckland, New Zealand, and a hundred places in between, with a sense of pride. For I was a Royal Navy sailor and I have sailed the 'seven seas' in times of war, and also in times of peace as part of the Merchant Navy. I have braved German U-boats, surface ships and the Luftwaffe in the harshest of conditions, escorting convoys on board HMS *Milne* and HMS *Savage* during the Second World War, taking vital supplies to the Soviet Union in our fight against the Nazis.

The Arctic convoys and the war in the Barents Sea have gone largely unrecognized over the years, to a point where the new generation are unaware that they actually happened.

This is wrong.

Since the days of Nelson, the sailors of this country have been used to being feted during wars and times of need, then being forgotten and ignored in times of peace.

So with little support apart from the local papers in Portsmouth and Yorkshire, a group of some 250 Arctic veterans in their eighties, and dependants of deceased Arctic veterans, with good wishes and encouragement from New Zealand, Australia, America, Canada and Nova Scotia, paraded up Whitehall on Saturday, 15 May 2004, and presented a petition, signed by 44,000 people to 10 Downing Street for Prime Minister Tony Blair's attention. The object of it was to gain recognition for the four-year campaign in the Arctic Barents Sea. Not a single report of the occasion appeared in national newspapers, or on TV.

The MoD was quickly on the ball, trotting out their usual excuse that the Arctic campaign was covered by the issue of the Atlantic Star.

Since when has the Barents Sea been in the Atlantic Ocean?

The fact is that ninety-eight ships ended up at the bottom of the Barents Sea, and Arctic conditions ensured that less than ten minutes in that sea meant death from exposure, even if rescued. Not to mention twenty-four hours of continuous daylight in summer, attacks from dive bombers and squadrons of torpedo bombers, and, when darkness did fall, the U-boats lurking silently below as the convoys approached. They would surface inside and play havoc with the slow moving merchant ships, while others picked off any 'tail-end Charlies' unable to keep up.

Mountainous seas of 40–50ft were commonplace, and decks frozen like skating rinks made the dash to 'action stations' a risk in itself. There was only a fifty-fifty chance of reaching Murmansk, and when finally you did get there and sat down to the first hot meal in a fortnight, guess what? 'Action stations' sounded again, and the enemy aircraft came over to bomb the survivors at anchor.

Now all you have to do is the return trip. A repeat of the same experience as before!

In the seventy-odd years since, we have had war films of the jungle, the desert, Monte Cassino in mountainous Italy, and of course the D-Day battles of France and Germany. We wait in vain for a film based on the Russian convoys and the tales my shipmates can tell about 'Saving Able Seaman Smith!'

In June 1942, the brand new destroyer HMS *Milne* left John Brown's Yard in Clydebank in her gleaming white and green camouflage, to undertake her trials off the Isle of

Arran. The film crew who joined us taking shots of the ship and gun crews for the film *In Which We Serve*, starring Richard Attenborough, then disembarked before we sailed for Scapa Flow. Too bad. They missed all the fun of PQ18, the most heavily attacked convoy of the whole campaign. Now that would have made a real blockbuster!

Perhaps if these desk-bound civil servants had also been present they would not have been in such a rush to turn down a medal, an Arctic Star that every man who sailed North of the Arctic Circle thoroughly deserved, just as much as a Burma Star, a North African Star, an Italy Star. It was only in 2012 that the government agreed to the award of the Arctic Star, just sixty-seven years too late!

Out of four years' actual sea service I spent four months in the Mediterranean, four months in and around the Atlantic and four months supporting the D-Day landings. This meant a medal for each. However, for over two years spent in far more dangerous and hazardous Arctic waters – both physically and mentally exhausting, and tragically fatal for the crews of the many merchant ships lost who died horrible deaths in freezing oil-covered Arctic waters, to say nothing of a few survivors who unbelievably told us that losing their ships meant their pay was stopped immediately, to them and their dependants back home – no medals!

These are the men those wearing white berets were representing in Whitehall on that day in 2004; the unknown, unsung heroes of the Russian convoys who deserved recognition for their service in the Barents Sea, not the Atlantic Ocean.

*   *   *

One day I received a phone call from the Russian Embassy inviting me to a medal ceremony aboard HMS *Belfast*, to receive the Ushakov Medal.

My friend Austin, also from the Russian Convoy Club, who suffered from poor eyesight, needed someone to accompany him. He was a Navy-trained DEMS (Defensively Equipped Merchant Ships) gunner who served on merchant ships. His exploits with a Russian convoy (PQ13) on the SS *Induna* ended when he was torpedoed and bombed, the ship was set on fire, and he spent four days adrift in the Barents Sea before being rescued by a Russian ship. He had the most harrowing experience of seeing several of his shipmates perish as each day passed.

Setting off on the journey to London in our blazers and white hats, it was not long before Austin, who was occupying an aisle seat, got chatting to someone opposite, who asked him where we were going. One thing led to another, and he ended up regaling him with his story! The four people across the aisle were all interested, and I realized the people in the carriage seats on either side had suddenly stopped their chatter and were listening too. On completion of his story he received a round of applause from half the carriage!

Arriving at Kings Cross, even the police at the end called us 'Gentlemen'!

The next day, Friday, 9 May 2014, together with some nineteen shipmate veterans who had all served on the Russian convoys, we attended the Merchant Navy Memorial before travelling to HMS *Belfast* on the River Thames, where we were warmly greeted by Russian veterans.

Leaving the ship after the ceremony I was handed a large carrier bag containing a framed picture of Admiral Ushakov and a brochure about the Admiral who, in thirty-five encounters, never lost a battle or a ship! He is held in the same esteem as Lord Nelson is in Britain. We were also given a certificate signed by President Putin, a bottle of Russian vodka and a handsome tankard.

Deciding to return to our hotel near Tower Hill for a meal, we encountered a young couple who were most interested in our visit and the reason for it. Before leaving they highly recommended a pub just around the corner, which my shipmate and I decided to try. To my amazement, outside the pub were about sixty people celebrating the end of their working week, and there was no room inside. We spent some time talking to an Australian and a friend, as there seemed no possibility of getting into the pub. However, they told us that upstairs there was a proper restaurant and so we entered to try it out.

On climbing the stairs we found a room empty except for a table with one gentleman and four ladies. Still wearing our white berets, we found a table for two and an extremely helpful waitress. I ordered a glass of house wine and my friend ordered a beer.

Suddenly the gentleman with the four ladies came over to our table and shook our hands. Crouching down to our level he said, 'Thank you for what you did for my country during the war.'

He was Russian.

I told him my country owed the Russian people a huge debt for their sacrifices, without which we would all be speaking German! After a few questions about our visit he resumed his seat and we found he had paid for an extra drink for us. I went across to thank him and was introduced to his wife and three lady friends. A really kind gesture, I thought.

While we were still having our meal, they got up to leave and we said goodbye. As his party left we were talking about how much we had enjoyed our two-day trip to London.

On asking for the bill to pay for our meal, the waitress replied there was no charge. It had been paid by the gentleman who had just left!

Individually, as veterans, we have always been treated as VIPs by the Russian people, and the award of the Ushakov medal on Victory Day, 9 May 2014, made it the most memorable day of my life!

The Ushakov medal, together with its citation, is a true campaign medal, and I feel it adequately makes up for my three years escorting convoys to Archangel and Murmansk on the two destroyers, HMS *Milne* and HMS *Savage*.